Valley Vegetables

Recipes for Forty of the Pioneer Valley's Vegetables

Claire Hopley

Photographs by Robert Hopley

To Shanti —
Happy Cooking,
Claire Hopley

Copyright © 2012 Claire Hopley
Published by Levellers Press
Amherst, Massachusetts

ISBN 978-1-937146-11-5

To Rose Sacco, for all her help

Acknowledgments

I have been writing the Table Talk food column in the *Amherst Bulletin* for over two decades. That opportunity has brought with it numerous recipes and ideas from readers, and information and advice from the food producers of the Pioneer Valley. I want to thank them all, and also Nick Grabbe, Bonnie Wells, and now Kathleen Mellen, successively my editors at the *Bulletin*.

While they helped make this book possible, other people have been essential to getting it into print. My thanks to publisher Steve Strimer of Levellers Press who designed, laid-out, and did everything else necessary to transform my emailed text into a book. Steve happily discovered the 5-A-Day typeface for the initial capitals designed by Jimmy Smith.

Pauline Lannon, President of Atkins Country Market on West Street in Amherst kindly made space available and Paul Koslowski, Assistant Produce Manager, helped pick out vegetables so they could be photographed for the cover. I am grateful also to Mary Ellen Warchol of Stockbridge Farm in Deerfield, who has shared many recipes over the years, including one for carrots on page 31 and another for eggplant on page 52. My husband Bob has taken countless pictures of vegetables – those he's grown himself, those he's spotted in local markets, and those I've cooked up. Several of these illustrate the pages and back cover of this book. As ever, I appreciate all the work he has done to help me.

I thank Five Colleges Inc. for their support. For permission to quote from "Rutabagas: A Love Poem" from *Sundogs* (Parallel Press, 2006) I thank poet James Silas Rogers of St. Thomas University in Minnesota. My thanks also to Interlink Publishing Group of Northampton for permission to adapt the Iraqi Zucchini Cake with Cardomom from a recipe in their 2009 publication *The Iraqi Cookbook* by Lamees Ibrahim.

Introduction

We've all been there: standing in a summery garden or late-afternoon kitchen gazing at a gorgeous heap of vegetables yet asking What on earth am I going to do with them all?

This question never arises as vegetables come into their season because we are so thrilled to see them. What can be more exciting than to spot the first asparagus thrusting from the ground at the very end of April, or to stroll the first outdoor farmers' markets in May, stopping to buy wintered-over parsnips and infant greens? Every month brings its own excitement: the snap of pea pods and the luxuriant leafiness of lettuce and chard in June, the green beans and summer squash of July, and then the eye-candy colors of tomatoes, peppers eggplants, and pumpkins in high summer and fall. It's when a vegetable has been around for a bit and is still producing like mad that you may find yourself ferreting out ways to use it.

This book gives you 120 answers in the form of recipes for 40 alphabetically arranged vegetables, all of them grown right here in the Valley. Most of them are easy recipes from various countries and historical sources that can add something new to your table. Many feature vegetables in their traditional role as side dishes. But a lot are for main dishes in which vegetables command the spotlight, and some are for breakfast preludes or dessert finales. Vegetarians will find plenty of no-meat dishes; but this is not a vegetarian cookbook. The aim is to have something for everybody: for meat and fish lovers, for those who like to bake and those who adore confecting giant pots of soup or preserving the harvest as jars of chutney. In short, this book is for anyone who loves our local vegetables and wants to make the most of them.

Thoughts on Cooking Vegetables

Vegetables are generally easy to cook, but here are some thoughts on making things even easier.

Weighing Things

Many vegetable recipes don't demand exact amounts of each ingredient. Soups and casseroles, for example, happily receive a bit more of this and a bit less of that depending on what's available. But it's often useful to know how much your vegetables weigh. For example, if a recipe includes a sauce—as Cauliflower Cheese does for example—the sauce ingredients will be calculated for vegetables of a particular weight. The ratio of vegetables to preservative ingredients such as vinegar and sugar in chutney is also important. Then, too, what do we mean by 'a big cabbage' or 'a medium onion?' Clearly, one person's 'medium' can be another's 'big.' Kitchen scales make it easy to keep track of how much stuff you have, and while they are handy for cooking vegetables they are absolutely vital for baking so they are a good investment.

Choosing Black or White Pepper

Some time in the 1970s pepper mills became huge in size and popularity as we realized that freshly ground black pepper was more flavorful than the stuff that comes ready-ground in cans. One side effect was that white pepper, which can be ground from white peppercorns but usually comes as a fine beige powder, disappeared from many tables and kitchens. That's a pity because its heat lifts many dishes, and its paleness preserves the pristine appearance of pale sauces and soups as well as light-colored vegetables such as leeks, onions, parsnips, and fennel. For these uses it's a better choice than black pepper. On a vivid salad the aroma and speckles of fresh-ground black pepper are more exciting.

Black and white pepper come from the same plant but are processed differently. To make black pepper, the berries are picked when they are red and slightly unripe, and left in the sun until their skins are wrinkled and black. For white pepper the berries are left on the plant for longer. After harvesting they are soaked to remove the outer layers leaving just the whitish seed. Pepper is a native of Southeast Asia and now grows in many tropical countries. Specialty shops sell peppercorns identified by their region of origin. Among the most prized for their flavors are Tellicherry and Malabar from India, and Muntok and Lampong from Indonesia.

Toasting Nuts

Toasting nuts makes them golden and brings out their aromas and flavors. Green beans with toasted almonds are an old favorite, and toasted pine-nuts garnish several classic Italian vegetable dishes. But you don't have to stick with the classics. You can use toasted nuts to garnish many vegetable dishes. There are several ways to toast them.

In a frying pan: Use a small frying pan over low heat. Add a teaspoon of oil or butter. Add the nuts in a single layer, and cook, turning once or twice, until they are glistening and aromatic. Pale nuts such as almonds and pine nuts should turn golden brown; nuts such as walnuts and pecans should turn 2–3 shades darker. This takes 3–4 minutes depending on the nuts and the heat. Watch them all the time as all nuts can turn from golden brown to burnt in what seems like the blink of an eye.

In the oven: Put the nuts in a single layer in an oven-proof dish. Put them in an oven, preferably at 275 degrees. Toast for about 5 minutes or until they are golden-brown and aromatic. Check frequently to prevent burning. If your oven temperature is higher, they will cook faster but the risk of burning is greater, so really keep your eye on them.

In the microwave: Put the nuts in a single layer in a ceramic microwavable dish. Toast for one minute then check. Depending on the power and your oven they might be ready. If not add more time in small increments so you don't overcook them. The microwave is especially convenient for toasting sliced almonds and pine-nuts.

Squeezing Citrus Fruit

If you warm lemons, oranges, or limes before squeezing them the heat breaks down their cell walls so you get more juice. You can warm them in an oven, a microwave, or even on the back of the stove if the burners are on. Before warming them, stick them in a couple of places with a pointed knife. This will allow for expansion and prevent them bursting if you leave them too long. They need about 1 minute in a microwave, 3-4 minutes in a 350-degree oven, or 10 minutes or so on the back of the stove. Once they are warm, wear an oven mitt to squeeze them in case the juice is hot.

Making Cheese Sauce

Cheese flatters many vegetables. You can take advantage by garnishing dishes of asparagus, Swiss chard, leeks, tomatoes, and many other harvests with grated cheese. But for real indulgence nothing beats a cheese sauce. Here's a basic recipe that's enough for 4 servings of vegetables. It can be doubled or even tripled if necessary. Choose Gruyère if you want a velvety smooth mildly flavored sauce; choose a sharp or extra-sharp Cheddar for more distinctly cheesy flavor. Parmesan is a useful addition because its dryness helps the sauce absorb the richness of the Gruyere or Cheddar.

You can, of course, use other cheeses. Emmenthal or Jarlsberg can substitute for Gruyere, though they lack its superlative meltingness; English cheeses such as Cheshire, Double Gloucester, or Red Leicester can be used instead of Cheddar. Their orange color comes from annatto, a natural colorant made from the seed coating of berries from a South American tree. These orange cheeses produce appetizingly yellow cheese sauces. Feta adds its own special salty bite, and is common in Greek cheese sauces. Blue cheeses also bring distinctive flavor, though they make the sauce look greyish. The flavor of any cheese sauce is enhanced by adding a small amount of mustard powder or cayenne. You don't need a lot because you don't want to taste the spice; its job is simply to pique the flavor of the cheese.

Cheese Sauce

> 2 tablespoons grated Parmesan
> 2 cups grated Gruyere or extra-sharp or sharp Cheddar
> 3 tablespoons all-purpose flour
> 1 teaspoon dry mustard powder or small pinch cayenne (optional)
> 3 tablespoons butter
> 1 1/4 cups milk
> White pepper to taste

To make the sauce, mix the Gruyere or Cheddar and Parmesan. Set 2 tablespoon of this mixture aside for topping the dish. Mix the flour with the mustard or cayenne. Melt the butter in a saucepan; remove from the heat and stir in the flour mixture until you have a smooth stiff paste. Stir in about a quarter cup of the milk, then return the pan to the heat and gradually add the remaining milk, stirring all the time. As the sauce thickens whisk it to make it smooth. When it has boiled for a minute or two stir in all the cheese except that reserved for the topping. When it has melted, taste and add salt and white pepper as needed. Pour this sauce over the vegetables and sprinkle with the reserved cheese. Let brown under a preheated broiler if you like.

Buying Eggs

Lots of vegetables pair beautifully with eggs to make quick and nutritious dishes. Asparagus, mushrooms, peppers, spinach and many other vegetables taste delightful when tucked into an omelet or frittata. Fried or poached eggs are good with potatoes and vegetable mixtures such as pepperonata and ratatouille. Hard-boiled eggs appear in some vegetable gratins such as Anglesey Eggs (page 71) and salads. Like most cookbooks this one follows the practice of using standard large eggs in the recipes. But if you love the rich fresh taste of the eggs you can buy from the many local producers who now have chickens pecking round their yards, you may find that a box of a dozen eggs contains eggs of 2 or 3 different sizes. It can be handy when you want just a little egg for using in breading fish or you'd like a big egg for breakfast, but in a baked item you need to be accurate. It helps to know that a large egg weighs 2 ounces. So if a recipe calls for 3 eggs, then you can mix and match eggs from a mixed-size box until you have 6 ounces in total.

Sterilizing Jars

Chutney and pickles should be packed into sterilized jars made from tempered glass. Canning jars made for vegetables or jam are suitable. The caps should be sterilized too. Do not use jars that are cracked or chipped. Nor should you re-use jars from store-bought preserves because high sterilizing temperatures can shatter them. Sterilize jars by washing them, filling them with hot tap water, then immersing them in a large pan (such as a canning bath or pasta pan) filled with hot water. Ensure that the water covers them by at least an inch. Boil them for 10 minutes. They will remain sterile as long as they are in the water, even when the water cools. If you take them out while they are hot, use tongs. Boil the lids too. Dry the jars with a freshly laundered cloth and fill as soon as you take them from the water. While pickles and chutneys that you plan to store for several months should be canned, those that are intended for use over a period of a few weeks do not need canning as the large amounts of vinegar as well as the sugar and salt in these condiments preserves them as long as they are kept in cold conditions.

Valley Vegetables
A to Z

Acorn Squash is a handsome racing-green creature, which slices into two scalloped vessels of golden flesh begging to be filled with something good. The flesh of acorn squash is dense, not watery or stringy, and its flavor is mild and sweet so it makes soothing soups and attractive side dishes. Its wavy edge and ample cavity make it the ideal squash for stuffing. Like other winter squashes, acorn survives for many weeks – months even – without rotting, but its taste and texture deteriorate, so this is a squash to eat quite soon after harvest.

ACORN SQUASH WITH CUMIN-PERFUMED LAMB AND LENTILS

This recipe evokes the aromas of a Middle Eastern spice market. The stuffing can be used with butternut and other squashes too.

> *2 acorn squashes, each about 1 1/2 – 2 pounds*
> *1/3 cup lentils, rinsed*
> *1 bay leaf*
> *salt to taste*
> *1/2 pound ground lamb*

Leverett farmstand with acorn squash and other vegetables

1 medium onion, chopped
2 garlic cloves, minced
1 teaspoon cumin seeds, or more to taste
1/2 teaspoon cinnamon
1/2 teaspoon al1spice
1 cup peeled, seeded and diced tomatoes
2 tablespoons chopped fresh parsley
Freshly ground black pepper
2 tablespoons toasted pine-nuts (see page ix)

Turn the oven to 425 degrees. Cut the squashes in half. Scoop out and discard the seeds. Place the halves cut side down on a baking tray lined with parchment paper or greased aluminium foil. Bake for about 45 minutes or until a skewer poked into the flesh meets no resistance. Remove and then enlarge the central cavity by scooping out some of the flesh and reserving it. Reduce the oven temperature to 350 degrees.

While the squash is cooking, put the lentils into a saucepan. Add enough cold water to cover them by 2 inches, half a teaspoon of salt and the bay leaf. Cover and bring to a boil. Simmer for 20-30 minutes or until they are tender. Drain and reserve them, discarding the bay leaf.

Meanwhile in a frying pan over medium heat, fry the ground lamb until it has browned and the fat has run from it. Scoop the meat out of the pan with a slotted spoon and set it aside. Add the chopped onion and garlic to the fat remaining in the pan and cook gently for 4-5 minutes. Add the cumin seeds and stir for a minute or until their fragrance perfumes the air. Now return the lamb and lentils to the pan; dust with the cinnamon and allspice, and fold in the tomatoes, half the parsley, and the reserved squash. Season with several grinds of black pepper plus salt to taste. Stir to mix everything together but avoid blending the mixture into a uniform mass.

Fill the squash halves with the lamb mixture, mounding it up. Cover lightly with foil and return to the oven, and cook for 8-10 minutes. (If it's more convenient, the stuffed squash halves can be kept covered in the fridge for up to 8 hours, then reheated just before serving) In this case they will take about 25 minutes to reheat). Sprinkle the pine nuts and remaining parsley on top just before serving. Serves 4.

ACORN SQUASH WITH SAGE AND APPLE STUFFING AND PECANS

The down-homey apple stuffing makes this a perfect partner to pork or duck dishes. Try it too with roast chicken.

> *2 Cortland, Delicious, or other firm apples, peeled and diced*
> *1 medium onion, peeled and chopped*
> *6 sage leaves*
> *2 tablespoons butter*
> *2 cups commercial stuffing crumbs such as Pepperidge Farm Herb Stuffing*
> *2 acorn squash, each about 1 1/2 pounds, halved and deseeded*
> *Salt and pepper to taste*
> *1/2 cup chopped pecans*

Preheat the oven to 425 degrees and grease a shallow pan in which the squash halves will sit without wobbling. Put the apples, onion, and two torn sage leaves into a medium saucepan and add enough water to cover by a quarter inch. Bring to simmering point, cover, and simmer for 10-15 minutes or until the apples and onion are tender. Stir in the butter, and then the stuffing crumbs. Add more hot water to the mixture if necessary to make a moist but not sloppy stuffing. Season the cut surfaces of the squash with salt and pepper then pile the stuffing into the hollows of each half. Put them in the greased dish, cover the dish lightly with foil, and bake for about 60–70 minutes or until the squash is tender. (If you have something else in the oven cooking at a lower temperature, you can still cook your squash at the same time, though at a lower temperature it will take longer to cook). Remove the foil for the last 10 minutes of cooking time and sprinkle the pecans on top of the stuffing. For serving garnish with the remaining sage leaves. Serves 4.

Other recipes: Try acorn squash instead of butternut squash in the recipes for Butternut Caribé, Butternut and Peanut Soup, and Butternut Sauté with Apples and Onions on pages 21–24. For a rice stuffing try Raisin and Walnut Pilaf in the stuffed peppers recipes on page 94.

A rugula is a springtime favorite in Europe. English settlers brought it to Massachusetts, where it thrived with its English name "rocket." It went out of fashion in the early twentieth century, but the 1980s love affair with all things Italian brought it back with its Italian name "arugula." Its vibrant mustardy bite distinguishes it from other small salad leaves, which are often tasteless.

GREEK ARUGULA AND CARROT SALAD WITH CAPERS AND OLIVES

In Greece arugula is called *rokka*. It arrives in late February and early March, and as soon as it's available, restaurants start serving it in their standard house salad, frequently teaming it with shredded carrots as in this recipe. After about 6 weeks, the weather gets too hot for arugula. Ask for a salad of *rokka* in May, and the waiter will make dramatic slashing movements with his hands and say, "Finished!"

> about 4–6 cups washed arugula
> 1 1/2 cups shredded carrots
> 2 tablespoons olive oil
> 1 tablespoon lemon juice
> 1/2 teaspoon Dijon mustard
> 1–2 teaspoons drained capers
> about 1 dozen Kalamata olives
> 1 slice of red onion separated into circles

Put the arugula and about one third of the carrots in the salad bowl. Whisk together the olive oil, lemon juice and Dijon mustard, Pour this over the arugula and carrots and toss. Mound the remaining carrots in the center and scatter the capers and olives on them. Finally, arrange the onion circles on top. Serves 4–6. (See illustration on back cover.)

ARUGULA AND PEARS WITH BLUE CHEESE

This dish is based on one called Lockets Savoury, which is an English appetizer made with watercress, pears and Stilton. It's delicious, but it can leave you so replete that it robs you of appetite for the main dish. So serve this as for a weekend lunch or add a vegetable dish and serve it for supper.

2 large ripe Bartlett pears, peeled, cored and cut in 6 slices each
squeeze lemon juice
2 tablespoons butter
1–2 tablespoons light-flavored olive oil
1/2 teaspoon dried thyme or oregano
6 slices of thick-cut whole wheat bread or 12 pieces of Italian bread
3 cups washed, dried and picked-over arugula
6–8 ounces of a New England blue cheese such as Great Hill Blue

As you peel and core the pears, squeeze the lemon juice on them to prevent them going brown. In a frying pan in which the pear slices will fit in a single layer, melt 1 tablespoon of the butter and a tablespoon of the oil. Lightly sauté the pears in this until they are golden and tender but not soft or falling apart. This takes 3–5 minutes.

Set the cooked pears on a plate. Add the remaining butter to the pear pan with the thyme. Lightly brush one side of the bread with this. (Should you think you won't have enough for all the bread – and the exact amount depends on the dimensions of your slices – add the additional tablespoon of oil as well.) Preheat the broiler and cover a baking sheet with foil or parchment paper. Put the prepared bread on the sheet. Cover each slice with the arugula, then a few pear slices. Crumble the blue cheese on top, using enough so that the arugula and pears are fairly well covered. Broil for 3–4 minutes, or until the cheese is melted and bubbling. Serve immediately. Serves 6.

Asparagus snares the senses. It invites you to pick it up, to admire its shaded purply point and firm stalk, and then to savor it, one luxurious bite at a time so you can revel in the satiny stem and the nubbliness of the folded tip. It tastes of springtime, of the very essence of baby leaves. Yet for all its striking individuality, asparagus partners other foods brilliantly. Jonathan Swift, author of Gulliver's Travels, wrote "O, 'tis a pretty picking with a tender chicken." He could well have added that it's also terrific with ham, with eggs, with salmon, with veal, and with lamb.

Asparagus enchants Valley residents because the rich loam of Hadley and surrounding villages is ideal for growing it – so ideal that from the 1930s to the 1970s it was America's premier asparagus region. Road signs hailed motorists with "Welcome to Hadley Asparagus Capital of the World." Then fusarium hit the soil. It makes asparagus give up their struggle for glory. Many dispirited asparagus growers turned to other crops. A few hung on though. They planted newly developed disease-resistant varieties. Now their asparagus no longer travels very far, but they grow enough for the Valley. The first bundles appear in front yards and farmstands in very late April and the last of them are still around in early June. No asparagus ever tastes as good as this local crop. The best way to enjoy it is to have your own asparagus festival when it's in season and eat it in as many ways as possible. For breakfast dip a few spears to dip into a soft-boiled egg or fold steamed tips into scrambled eggs or an omelet. For lunch, spread hummus on a bagel and put cooked and cooled asparagus on top. And at supper, asparagus steals the show, whether it stars in a main dish or shines in splendid isolation on the side. Then for dessert you can have asparagus ice-cream. It's made by Beth Cook at Flayvors of Cook's Farm on South Maple Street in Hadley for the May–June asparagus season.

ASPARAGUS IN JACKETS

Snuggled into a puff pastry jacket asparagus looks spiffy enough to serve with party drinks. For a springtime supper make 4 or 5 per person and serve with a salad such as the Greek Arugula and Carrot Salad with Capers and Olives on page 4 or the Spinach and Radish Salad on page 112. You can wrap the asparagus in slices of both ham and cheese, or just one or the other if you prefer. (See back cover for illustration.)

16 thick stalks asparagus
1 package frozen store-bought puff pastry
2 tablespoons mayonnaise
16 thin slices ham
16 slices Swiss cheese

Trim off the woody ends of the asparagus stalks. Bring to boil a frying pan of lightly salted water. Drop the asparagus into it, and simmer for 1–2 minutes, or until it feels just tender when prodded with a fork. Remove with a slotted spoon, cool, and pat dry with paper towel.

Follow the maker's directions for unfreezing the pastry. Preheat the oven to 400 degrees. Cover a baking sheet with parchment paper or grease it. Roll each sheet of pastry to stretch it a little. Use a pastry brush to spread the asparagus stalks – not the tips – with mayonnaise. Roll each one in a cheese slice then a ham slice or just one or the other, then in enough pastry to cover it, leaving the tip exposed. Seal the pastry seam by brushing it with cold water. Place seam side down on the baking sheet. Bake for 18–20 minutes or until golden and crisp. Serves 4 with a salad, or 6–8 if served with drinks.

ASPARAGUS WITH CHIVEBLOSSOM VINAIGRETTE

By mid-May the asparagus season is at its height, and the chive clumps are stretching their pompom blossoms to the sun. These mauve flowers taste just like chive leaves, though a little milder. They look and taste lovely with asparagus in this simplest of side dishes.

1 teaspoon Dijon mustard
2 tablespoons olive oil
1–3 teaspoons white wine or cider vinegar
Salt to taste
1 bunch asparagus, woody stems trimmed
6 chiveblossoms plus extra blossoms for garnish
2 teaspoons snipped chives

In a small bowl, whisk together the mustard, olive oil, a teaspoon of vinegar, and a pinch of salt. Taste to see if you would like a saltier or sharper dressing; if so add a pinch more salt or a little more vinegar, tasting after each addition until the taste is as you like it.

Bring a shallow pan of water to the boil and add 1/2 teaspoon of salt. Put in the asparagus and cook for 3–5 minutes, depending on the thickness of the stems. Check for tenderness by prodding them with a fork. Remove from the water, and quickly pat off excess moisture with paper towel. Put them on a shallow serving dish. Tear the petals from 6 chiveblossoms, and add most of them to the dressing along with most of the snipped chives. Pour it over the warm asparagus and turn the asparagus gently in it. Sprinkle the remaining petals and chives on top. Let cool to room temperature. For serving garnish with whole blossoms. Serves 4–6.

SALMON AND ASPARAGUS BISQUE

Chefs have taken to serving prime portions of fish or meat in a pool of flavorful broth. Here the green asparagus bisque shows off the pink salmon in a dish that celebrates spring.

> *1 bunch asparagus, about 16 stalks, washed*
> *1 medium leek, washed*
> *2 tablespoons butter*
> *1 6-inch stick celery*
> *4 stems parsley*
> *1 sprig of thyme*
> *salt, pepper and sugar to taste*
> *4 pieces salmon fillet, each about 6 ounces*
> *pea shoots or parsley or both for garnish*

Cut off the woody asparagus bottoms and discard them. Cut off the tips, and put them in pan. Pour on 2 cups boiling water. Simmer for two minutes, then drain, reserving the liquid. Drop the tips into cold water, and when they are cool transfer them to the fridge.

Cut the asparagus stalks into 5-cm (2-inch) pieces. Slit the leek longways and rinse under water to make sure it has no soil in it. Cut into matchsticks. Melt the butter in a large saucepan, and stir in the leeks. Season lightly with salt, and let them sweat over low heat for 2–3 minutes. Add the asparagus stalks, cook for another 2 minutes, and then put in the celery, 2 stems of the parsley, thyme, and the liquid reserved from cooking the asparagus tips plus salt to taste. Liquid should cover the vegetables by at least 2 inches, so add more water if necessary. Simmer for 15 minutes or until the asparagus and celery are soft. Discard the celery and thyme. Pour the mixture into a food processor, in batches if necessary, and process until completely smooth. Return to the rinsed-out pan and set aside while you cook the salmon.

Place the salmon in a lidded frying pan or other shallow pan with the fish or chicken stock, or lightly salted water and the remaining 2 stems of parsley, Cover and simmer on top of the stove. Keep it at a gentle simmer for 5–7 minutes, or until it has cooked through. Meanwhile, bring the asparagus mixture back to simmering point. Also reheat the asparagus tips by giving them 30 seconds in a microwave or dropping them in boiling water for 30 seconds.

Remove the cooked salmon filets to the center of warmed pasta bowls or soup plates and keep warm. Strain the poaching liquid from the salmon into the asparagus mixture, and stir it over high heat. Taste and season with salt, pepper, and a pinch or two of sugar. When it has simmered for 1–2 minutes, ladle it around — not on — the salmon. Garnish the salmon with pea shoots or parsley and the reheated asparagus tips. Serves 4.

ASPARAGUS AND HAM GRATIN

This gratin is quite hearty – good for one of those cool or rainy spring evenings that remind us that summer is still to come.

> *12 thick stems of asparagus, washed and trimmed*
> *Salt to taste*
> *12 thin slices well-flavored ham such as Black Forest ham*
> *Cheese sauce (see page xi)*
> *1–2 tablespoons grated Parmesan*

    Preheat the oven to 350 degrees. Drop the asparagus into a shallow pan of boiling salted water and cook for 4 minutes after the water returns to simmering point. Remove it from the water into a bowl of chilled water to reduce its temperature. Pat dry with paper towels then wrap a slice of ham around each stalk. Transfer to a greased rectangular pan just big enough to fit them all packed side by side. Pour the cheese sauce on top and sprinkle the Parmesan on the surface. Bake for 15 minutes or until the top is golden. Let rest for 5 minutes before serving. Alternately, you can prepare it ahead of time, keeping it covered in the fridge for up to 6 hours before proceeding to bake it. Add the Parmesan just before baking. Since it starts out cold, the baking time will be 10 minutes longer. Serves 4.

    Other recipes: Use asparagus cut into 2-inch pieces instead of sugar-snap peas in the Risotto with Sugar-snap Peas and Spring Herbs on page 90.

Beets look homely when they come out of the ground: all dusty with ragged leaves drooping from maroon stems. But once they are cooked and peeled, they gleam like precious stones. The color is the thing to watch. It dyes (and flavors) everything else in the dish. Food producers take advantage of this by using beet juice to tint raspberry yogurt pink and to make commercial jam look appetisingly red. A favorite Polish condiment Horseradish with Beets also looks rosily pink. It's made from roughly equal amounts of horseradish and grated cooked beets seasoned with salt and sugar, and drizzled with vinegar.

ROASTED BEETS WITH LEMON AND DILL

Though almost all beets are eye-candy purple, some farmers and gardeners also grow orange and yellow beets. If possible include one or two of these in this recipe for the jazzy color contrast. Use medium beets for this recipe; big ones take too long to cook and little ones don't yield enough.

Roasted Beets with Lemon and Dill

6–8 beets
1 tablespoon chopped dill
2 lemons
Salt to taste
Dill springs for garnish

Preheat the oven to 400 degrees. Cut off and discard all but the last 2 inches of the beet stems. Wash the beets; dry with paper towels and wrap each one in foil. Bake them for an hour or until tender when poked with a skewer. (If you also want to cook something else that requires a lower temperature, go ahead. The beets will cook just fine though at lower temperatures they take longer).

Let the cooked beets cool until you can handle them, then slip off the skins and the remains of the stems. Cut the beets into chunks and toss with the chopped dill. Arrange on a shallow dish. Using a lemon zester, scrape thin strings of zest from a lemon. Halve the lemon and squeeze the juice of half of it on the beets. Garnish with the zest strings and dill sprigs. Cut the remaining lemon in wedges and serve at the side for people to use if they want a lemonier flavor. Serves 4–8.

BABY BEET SALAD

This salad is one of the commonest ways of serving beets in Greece. It makes good use of their leaves. Often people who find beets too strongly flavored enjoy the milder taste of the leaves, so this salad has something for everyone.

2 bunches of baby beets with their leaves
salt to taste
3/4 teaspoon allspice or more to taste
3 tablespoons olive oil
1–2 teaspoons oregano
1 big lemon cut into wedges

Cut the leaves from the beets, leaving about 2 inches of stalk on the beet. Put the beets in a large pan of water and simmer until tender, which takes about 40 minutes or longer for larger beets. While they are cooking sort the leaves, discarding any coarse or discolored outer leaves and just keeping the tender springier inner ones. Drop them into a pan of boiling salted water and cook for about 20 minutes or until tender. Crispness is not desirable here, so cook for longer if necessary. Drain the leaves well. Dust about half the allspice on a plate or in a bowl and dump on the leaves. Sprinkle the rest of the allspice on top and then toss so the allspice flavors all the leaves. Pour on a tablespoon or more of olive oil and let stand at room temperature. To test the beets for doneness poke with a fork. When tender, drain, cool enough to handle them, then peel. Leave tiny beets whole; cut bigger ones in halves or quarters. Season with salt and then toss with oil and oregano. Put them on the same plate as the leaves, either alongside or in a circle. Add lemon wedges for squeezing over the salad and serve at room temperature. Serves 4–6.

BEET AND BARLEY RISOTTO

2/3 cup pearl barley
6–7 medium beets (about 1 pound), cooked
2 tablespoons butter
1/3 cup chopped shallot or onion
1 bay leaf
3/4 cup red wine
1 teaspoon powdered allspice
About 2–3 cups hot vegetable or chicken broth
Salt and pepper to taste

Put the pearl barley in a bowl and cover it plentifully with water. Set aside for an hour (no problem if you leave it longer), stirring once or twice. Drain it. Grate or chop half the beets. Cut the remainder into bite-size wedges or cubes.

In a medium frying pan or sauté pan, melt the butter over moderate heat. Stir in the chopped onion and let it soften for 3–4 minutes, then stir in the drained barley. Add the wine and bay leaf, lower the heat and simmer for 5–6 minutes over moderate heat until most of the wine has evaporated. Now add half a cup of the broth, season with salt and a little pepper, and continue cooking over moderate heat until the liquid has been mostly absorbed. Add another half cup of broth and cook, stirring from time to time, until it has also been absorbed. The barley should now be somewhat softened. Add another half cup of broth along with the chopped beats, and the allspice. Stir to mix everything well together, and cook until the liquid has been almost absorbed again. Taste to check the seasoning and the tenderness of the barley. It should be tender and a little chewy but not hard in the middle of the grain. If it is not ready, add more broth and continue cooking until the right texture is reached. When this happens, fold in the diced beets and cook with the lid on the pan for 3-4 minutes or just until the beets are heated through.

Discard the bay leaf before serving. Serves 4–6 as a side dish.

Broccoli tastes blah or bitter when it has been long out of the ground, which means that fresh local broccoli tastes entirely different from the huge broccoli heads that reach the supermarkets from far away. We see a lot of broccoli doing journeyman work as a companion to meat and fish dishes, but it can also take command in pasta dishes and quiches. And with their deep color and multiple crannies, raw broccoli florets are just the thing for dunking into creamy party dips.

BROCCOLI AND CHEDDAR SOUP

This thick soup is perfect for lunch. You can make variations by using other cheeses. Gruyere is creamier and mild. Emmenthal or Jarlsberg are other mild cheeses that work well, while a Pepper Jack adds a jolt of heat.

> *2 tablespoons canola or other vegetable oil*
> *1 small onion, chopped*
> *4-inch stalk celery, chopped*
> *1 pound broccoli florets with stems but not leaves*
> *5 cups chicken or vegetable stock*
> *Salt to taste*
> *1 tablespoon flour*
> *2 teaspoons dry mustard powder (optional)*
> *1 cup milk or half and half*

4 tablespoons grated Parmesan
*2 cups (4 ounces) grated sharp Cheddar cheese plus
    more for serving*
White pepper to taste

Heat the oil in a large saucepan. Add the chopped onion and celery, and cook gently for 3–4 minutes. Add the broccoli florets and the stock with half a teaspoon of salt. Simmer for 15 minutes or until the broccoli is completely tender.

Let cool for a few minutes then process in batches in a food processor, and return to the pan.

In a small bowl mix the flour and mustard; add 2–3 tablespoons of the milk and stir to a paste. Thin this down with about half a cup of milk then stir it into the broccoli mixture. Add the remaining milk then bring to simmering point and simmer for 3-4 minutes, stirring occasionally. Off the heat, stir in the Parmesan and Cheddar. Return to a very low heat and stir until the cheese has melted and the soup has just reached simmering point. Taste and add more salt if needed (the cheese may have provided enough), and pepper if liked. Serves 6–8.

BROCCOLI CREAM

This is one of those recipes that lends itself to multiple uses. Most obviously you can toss it with pasta. With only a final sprinkle of Parmesan, this makes an instant supper dish — though you can add some sautéed mushrooms or ham bits if you want a contrast. You can also use Broccoli Cream as a spread on bread or in party canapés. If you want a dip for dunking raw vegetables, thin it with a little sour cream, plain yogurt, or milk.

*12 ounces broccoli (to make about 4–5 cups broccoli
    florets)*
Salt and pepper to taste
3 ounce package cream cheese
Freshly grated nutmeg to taste
1 tablespoon olive oil or butter

Wash the broccoli and break into florets. Drop them in a pan of boiling water with half a teaspoon of salt and cook for 6–7 minutes or until tender. Drain and pat dry with paper towels. Mash the broccoli or process it in a food processor or blender, then add the cream cheese, and mix it in. Taste and season with salt, pepper, and freshly grated nutmeg to taste. This will sauce enough pasta for 3–4 people, or lots more if served it as a party dip with raw vegetables or pita chips.

BROCCOLI RED PEPPER AND ROSEMARY QUICHE

The first broccoli generally comes in late June – way before the red pepper harvest, so if you are making this quiche early in the year use extra broccoli and just a few of the red pepper strips that come in jars from Italy or Spain. In August and September, broccoli plants are still putting out shoots as red peppers are flaunting their scarlet so you can up the quantity of pepper strips. Chose broccoli florets that have a nice head plus some stem so they look like mini trees.

> *1 home-made or store-bought shortcrust pie shell*
> *About 6–8 ounces broccoli florets*
> *1 1/2 cups grated Vermont extra-sharp Cheddar*
> *1/4 teaspoon dried rosemary*
> *8 strips cooked red pepper*
> *Salt and pepper to taste*
> *4 eggs*
> *1 3/4 cups whole milk*

Preheat the oven to 400 degrees. Have the prepared pie-shell in a metal or tempered glass deep-dish pie pan or quiche dish. Prick the base, cover it with aluminium foil, and weight it down with dried beans or small coins. Bake for 20 minutes or until the surface is completely dry.

While the shell is baking, drop the broccoli florets into boiling salted water and let them cook for just 2 minutes. Remove and cool under cold running water. Pat dry with paper towel.

Preheat the oven to 425 degrees. Scatter the grated cheese over the pie crust. Arrange the broccoli attractively on top and sprinkle with rosemary. Place the strips of red pepper in a spoke pattern so they will mark 8 divisions in the quiche. Whisk the eggs and milk together, add pepper and just a little salt (the cheese is already salted so you won't need much). Pour this gently into the dish. If necessary rearrange the broccoli and red pepper strips to make them attractive. Bake for 10 minutes, then reduce the temperature to 350 degrees and bake for 10–15 minutes longer or until a knife blade slid into the center comes out clean. Cool. Serve at room temperature. Serves 6–8. (Illustrated on back cover.)

BROCCOLI RABE WITH BALSAMIC VINEGAR AND CRANBERRIES

Broccoli rabe is also called, raab, rapini, and broccoletti. The last name identifies it as a small form of broccoli. Its head are no more than the size of quarter, and the business end of the plant is really the stem and leaves. They taste more dramatic than their big-headed relative: slightly bitter and peppery: just what's needed to stand up to the sweet-sour flavors of this dish. In Italy, raisins would be used; this version gets a Massachusetts twist with dried cranberries. Another way to serve broccoli rabe is to steam it, then toss it over medium heat with a fruity olive oil and a pinch of red pepper flakes.

3 tablespoons dried cranberries
1 large bunch broccoli rabe (about 1 pound)
Salt to taste
3 tablespoons fruity olive oil
Pinch red pepper flakes
1 tablespoon balsamic vinegar plus more for serving
2 tablespoons toasted almonds (see page ix)

Put the cranberries in enough warm water to cover them by one inch and let them soak for 20–30 minutes.

Wash the broccoli rabe, trim the ends of the stalks and discard any withered or battered leaves. Bring a large pan of water to the boil, add half a teaspoon of salt and drop the broccoli rabe in it. Let it return to the boil and cook for 3 minutes, then drain. Blanch the broccoli rabe by running cold water on it. Drain again and pat with paper towel to soak up excess water.

Heat the olive oil in a frying pan. Add the broccoli rabe and sprinkle with the pepper flakes, drained cranberries, and then the vinegar. Cook over moderate heat for 2 minutes, gently turning over the broccoli rabe just once or twice so not to break it. For serving sprinkle with a little extra balsamic vinegar if you like, and scatter the toasted almonds on top. Serves 4–6.

Other recipes: Stir-Fried Chicken with Snowpeas and Broccoli (page 89)

Brussels sprouts sometimes appear on English Christmas cards because they are must-have partners to the Christmas turkey or goose. Indeed, in Britain they are one of the best-loved (and cheapest) winter vegetables. Locally, though, they rival beets and parsnips in the love 'em or hate 'em league. Those who don't much like them may be tempted by their German name: *der Rosenkohl* – literally rose-cabbage. They really are the size of roses and almost as pretty.

BRUSSELS SPROUTS WITH CHESTNUTS AND NUTMEG

Brussels sprouts vary in size and the small ones cook faster than big ones, so ideally choose those that are similar in size. For this dish medium to large sprouts are best because they contrast with the smaller chestnut pieces.

2 pounds Brussels sprouts
4 tablespoons butter
1/3 cup white wine
1 cup vacuum-packed, canned, or frozen chestnuts
grated nutmeg

Trim off the bottom of the stalk of each sprout, and with it, any floppy or damaged exterior leaves. Cut criss-cross slashes in the base of the stalk. Cut each chestnut in half or into three if it is especially large.

Bring a large pan of salted water to the boil. Drop the Brussels sprouts into it, and simmer for about 6–8 minutes until they have softened a little but are still firm. Drain.

In a shallow pan, preferably one that can be taken to the table, melt the butter. When it is has white bubbles round the edges, pour in the wine and let it bubble away for a couple of minutes. Grate in a little nutmeg then add the chestnut pieces and the Brussels sprouts. Stir gently to coat them with the butter. It's fine if the chestnuts break into bean-size pieces but don't let them disintegrate into mush. Let them reheat over a low burner if necessary. Season with freshly grated nutmeg and serve immediately. Serves 8.

SOUP OF BRUSSELS SPROUTS WITH GOLDEN SIPPETS

When I saw Brussels Sprouts Soup with Golden Sippets on the menu of the Adelphi Hotel in Liverpool in the 1970s the mingling of the ordinary vegetable with fey golden sippets suggested something the Beatles might have conjured up. Later I discovered that sippets were hard pieces of bread served with the soups and stews of the Middle Ages and Renaissance. The golden sippets I had in Liverpool were enticingly crisp golden triangles of fried bread – a luxurious companion to the pale green soup. They hadn't been touched by the Beatles' magic or spangled by a fairy's wand, but they were delicious.

For the soup:

1 pound Brussels sprouts
2 shallots or a small onion, peeled and chopped
6-inch stick celery, chopped
1 small or medium carrot, peeled and halved
1 medium potato, peeled and diced
1 bay leaf
Salt, pepper, and freshly grated nutmeg to taste
About 1 cup milk
1 tablespoon cornstarch
Optional garnishes of chopped parsley or 1 teaspoon caraway seeds

For the Golden Sippets:

3 tablespoon butter
1 tablespoon olive oil
4 square slices of white bread, crusts removed

Wash the Brussels sprouts; trim off any coarse or battered leaves. Bring 4 cups of water to a boil in a large saucepan. Drop in the Brussels sprouts along with the shallots or onion, the celery, carrot, potato, and bay leaf. Season lightly with salt, pepper, and freshly grated nutmeg, and put on the lid, leaving space for steam to escape. Simmer for 20 minutes or until the sprouts and potato are tender. Remove and discard the carrot and bay leaf. Let the mixture cool a little then process in batches or pass it through a food mill, and return it to the pan. To finish the soup, stir in the milk, and taste, adding nutmeg, pepper, and salt if necessary to adjust the seasoning. Return to the heat. Stir the cornstarch to a thin paste with about a quarter of cup of cold water; mix in some of the hot soup then stir it into the soup in the pan. Simmer for 3–4 minutes before serving.

Meanwhile, make the golden sippets. Heat the butter and oil in a frying pan over fairly high heat. Cut each slice of bread into two triangles. When the oil and butter mixture is foamy drop in as many of the bread triangles as will easily fit in your pan. Fry briskly on both sides until golden – about 1–2 minutes per side. Drain on paper towels.

Garnish the soup with chopped parsley or caraway seeds if you like. Serve two sippets per person on the side. (Actually people often want more so double the number of sippets if you are feeling reckless about calories.) Serves 4.

B | 21

Butternut doesn't have the prettiest color or the most alluring shape of the winter squash family, but its lack of convolutions makes it easier to peel than many of its cousins. Once you have stripped away is beige skin you have a long cylindrical chunk that can be cut into circles, semi-circles, or dice. You also have the bulbous end where the seeds live. Some people discard this end because it has less flesh, but it can be handy for stuffing. Simply scoop out the seeds, sit it upright, and pack its cup-shaped cavity with a filling of your choice.

BUTTERNUT CARIBÉ

Never ever let butternut or other squashes see water unless you are making soup. In water they just fall apart, abandoning texture and a lot of flavor. Baking chunks in the oven or microwave preserves the taste. Here the perfumes of two Caribbean products – nutmeg and rum – make mashed squash into something special.

*1 large butternut squash (about 2 pounds or a little
   more)*
salt to taste
2 tablespoons butter
2 tablespoons dark rum
freshly grated nutmeg

Cut the bulbous end off the butternut and remove and discard all the seeds and the fibres attached to them. (A melon baller is a good tool for cleaning out the last of the fibres.) Halve the remaining squash, and cut the straight end into large chunks. Cook the unpeeled butternut by one of the two following methods. Either put the chunks in a microwavable dish or plate, cover loosely with plastic wrap and microwave for about 10–12 minutes or until tender. Alternately, bake in a foil-covered dish in the oven at 350 degrees for about 45 minutes or until tender. (If you are cooking something else in the oven at a different temperature, you can put the butternut in at the same time, though at lower temperatures it will take longer to soften and at higher it will cook faster.) When done remove from the oven and let it cool until it is handleable. Peel off the skin.

Put the butternut in a food processor, in batches if necessary. Add the butter, the rum, and a little salt. Process until smooth. Alternately you can puree it in a blender or food mill, or simply mash it by hand. Grate in approximately 1/4 teaspoon nutmeg. Taste for seasoning and add more nutmeg and salt to taste. You might also want to increase the amount of rum a little. You need enough for a background flavor, but not so much that the flavor overwhelms that of the other ingredients. Serve immediately, or make up to a day ahead and reheat in a 350-degree oven or a microwave before serving. Serves 6.

BUTTERNUT AND PEANUT SOUP

This soup is easiest made very thick then diluted with stock or milk at serving time. Odd as it sounds, it's especially good diluted with evaporated milk. You could also convert this to Butternut Coconut Soup by omitting the peanut butter and diluting the soup with a can of light coconut milk. A zing of hot chili sauce goes especially well with the coconut variation. In winter I like a very hot bowl of this soup with a Rorschach splash of very cold heavy cream.

> *3 tablespoons olive oil or sunflower oil*
> *2 onions, chopped*
> *1 clove peeled garlic*
> *2 apples, peeled and chopped*
> *2–4 teaspoons curry powder or more to taste*
> *1 butternut squash weighing 2–3 pounds, peeled and cut in big chunks*
> *salt and pepper to taste*
> *2–3 tablespoons smooth peanut butter or more to taste*
> *milk or evaporated milk or light coconut milk for serving*
>
> *Optional garnishes for serving:*
> *Greek yogurt or sour cream*
> *Chopped parsley or cilantro*
> *Oyster crackers*

Heat the olive oil in a large pan and stir in the chopped onions and the garlic clove. Let them soften gently over low heat, then stir in the apples. After a further minute stir in the curry powder, using just 2 teaspoons if you want no more than a faint background flavor, and up to 4–5 teaspoons for a distinct curry taste. Add the chunks of butternut, sprinkle with a little salt, and then add enough water to cover all the ingredients. Stir, cover with a lid and bring to simmering point. After about 10 minutes add the peanut butter, again adjusting the amount to suit your taste. Continue simmering, stirring from time to time, until the butternut is completely soft. Cool to lukewarm. Process in batches in a food processor or food mill.

At this point you can freeze the soup, or simply return it to the pan and reheat with whatever amount of milk or other liquid you need to dilute it to the consistency you want. (It's at its best as a creamy fairly thick soup, rather than a thin one.) Also adjust the seasoning to your taste. Add a dollop of yogurt or sour cream plus a sprinkle of parsley or cilantro to each serving, or serve with parsley or cilantro plus oyster crackers. Makes 6–8 servings.

BUTTERNUT SAUTEED WITH APPLES AND ONIONS

This recipe derives from Robert May's directions for buttering 'gourds, pumpions, cucumbers or muskmelons' in his 1660 book *The Accomplish't Cook*. May's directions read: "Fry them in slices ... either floured or in batter, being fried serve them with beaten butter and vinegar, or beaten butter and juice of an orange." Cortland apples are perfect for this dish because they stay white even when peeled and cooked, and the slices hold their shape. Golden Delicious is another variety that holds shape and resists browning. Many other Valley-grown apples work well too, but avoid McIntoshes as cooking turns them to mush.

1 large butternut (about 2 pounds)
salt and pepper to taste
2–3 tablespoons plain flour
2 Cortland apples, peeled and cored
1 medium-large onion peeled, halved and sliced

> *3 tablespoons light-flavored oil such as canola or*
>   *grapeseed oil*
> *1 tablespoon butter*
> *1 tablespoon finely chopped fresh parsley*
> *1 large navel or other orange, cut in wedges*

You won't need the bulbous end of the butternut, so cut it off then slice the straight end into 1/2-inch thick. Cut in into half moons. Salt and pepper them lightly, then dust with flour. Cut each apple into 8 slices. Dust them lightly with flour.

Heat 2 tablespoons of the oil and the butter in a large frying pan over high heat; add the squash slices a few at a time and fry until the underside is golden and the edge tinged with brown. This takes 3–4 minutes. Turn and cook the other side. As the pieces become tender, remove them to a heated plate, and add the apple slices to the pan, letting these also fry to a light golden brown.

Meanwhile, in a tablespoon of the oil poured into a small frying pan over medium heat, gently fry the sliced onion until it turns golden but not brown. When the apples and butternut are done pile them on a serving dish and top with the onions and parsley. Squeeze on the juice from a couple of the orange wedges, and garnish with the remainder so people can add more juice if they like. Serves 6.

BUTTERNUT FRIES

The straight end of a butternut is easy to cut into French fry look-alikes, but because these fries are baked not fried, they don't have the fat and calories of traditional fries. You won't need the bulbous end in this recipe.

> *1 large butternut squash*
> *1–2 tablespoon flour*
> *1–2 tablespoons light olive oil or peanut oil*
> *salt to taste*
> *freshly grated black pepper or paprika or cayenne*
>   *pepper to taste*

Preheat the oven to 450 degrees and line a baking sheet with either aluminium foil or baking parchment.

Cut the bulbous end from the squash and reserve it for another purpose. Peel the straight part of the squash and cut it into strips about 1/2 inch wide and 4 inches long. Put them in a single layer on a chopping board and sift the flour over them through a sieve. Turn them so all surfaces are lightly dusted with the flour.

Place them in a single layer on the prepared pan, Drizzle with the oil and lightly sprinkle with salt. Bake for 15 minutes then flip over and bake for another 10 minutes or until they feel tender when pierced with a fork. For serving, you can lightly dust with pepper, paprika, or a tiny bit of cayenne if you like. Serves 4–6.

Other recipes: You could use the bulbous ends of butternut squash instead of acorn squash in the recipes for stuffed acorn squash on pages 1–3, or you could fill them with a pilaf such as the Carrot Pilaf on page 33. The straight end, sliced and cut into semi-circles, can be substituted for pumpkin in the Marinated Pumpkin Slices with Mint on page 105. Butternut also works in the Pumpkin Curd recipe on page 106, in the Tomato and Winter Squash Chutney on page 138, and Moroccan Seven-Vegetable Tagine on page 144.

Cabbage is one of the Pioneer Valley's great fall bargains. Farmstands and supermarkets sell huge tight heads of it for just a dollar or two, and since they weigh in at 12 pounds and more one cabbage can provide many meals. These cabbages are the white cabbages favored in the Polish community for making sauerkraut. They are still around in March for the St Patrick's Day meal of Corned Beef and Cabbage. Valley farmers also grow Savoy cabbage, whose crinkly leaves shade from palest primrose to darkest forest green. More elegant than its burly white cousin, it does not hold as well in the fridge, so eat it soon after purchase.

COLCANNON

Savoy is the best cabbage for making colcannon – a favorite Irish mixture of cabbage and potatoes. But white cabbage or kale are equally traditional.

> 1 1/2 pounds potatoes, peeled
> 5 tablespoons butter
> 1 1/2 pounds cabbage or kale, chopped
> Salt taste
> 1 medium leek or 6 scallions, washed and trimmed
> 1 cup milk
> 1/2 teaspoon mace or nutmeg
> Pepper to taste

Cook the potatoes in boiling salted water until tender, then drain and mash them with 2 tablespoons of the butter. While they are cooking fill another pan with water, add half a teaspoon of salt, bring to the boil, drop in the cabbage or kale, and boil until tender but not overdone – about 15 minutes. Drain and finely chop the cabbage or kale. Cut the leek or scallions into 1-inch bits, drop them in the milk and let simmer gently for about 8 minutes or until tender. Mix the cabbage or kale with the potatoes. Stir in the leeks or scallions and the milk they cooked in plus the mace or nutmeg and pepper. Mix well but not so much as to make a uniform mass. Reheat as necessary then put in a bowl, make a well in the center, melt the remaining butter and pour it in. Serves 6.

FAR I KAL

This classic dish is so precious to Norwegians that they argue about when it's at its best. The consensus favors it the second time around, but there's a constituency that votes for excellence only after the seventh reheating. It can't be made in small quantities so you will definitely have enough leftovers to taste it a second time; seven seems a bit ambitious. This dish is for lamb lovers as well as cabbage lovers.

> *5 pounds lean bone-in shoulder lamb chops*
> *4 pounds white cabbage, chopped in bite-size pieces*
> *Salt to taste*
> *1 tablespoon flour*
> *1 tablespoon black peppercorns*

Cut each lamb chop into 2 or 3 pieces. Discard any large pieces of fat but do not remove the bones. Put a third of the cabbage into a large pan and dust it lightly with salt and a teaspoon of flour. Add a few peppercorns. Put half the lamb on top. Season it with salt and scatter on a few peppercorns. Repeat this with another third of the cabbage, another teaspoon of flour, more peppercorns and the rest of the lamb. Top with the remaining cabbage, any leftover peppercorns, and a final teaspoon of flour. Pour in water until it comes just below the top of the cabbage. Put on the lid and cook over a very low heat until simmering. Continue simmering over a low heat or transfer to a 300-degreee oven and cook until the meat and cabbage are both very tender. This takes at least 2 hours; cooking longer is better. Serve with boiled potatoes and carrots or rutabaga. Serves 6.

RABBIT BRAISED WITH CABBAGE AND CARROTS

This casserole can be made ahead and reheated. Indeed, rabbit benefits from long cooking, which seems to enhance its flavor. If you can't stand the idea of eating rabbit, try this with bone-in chicken thighs.

2 rabbits, each cut in 6 pieces or 8 bone-in chicken thighs
salt and white pepper to taste
3 tablespoons all-purpose flour
2 tablespoons olive oil
1 tablespoon butter
6 cloves garlic,
1 1/2 cups chicken stock or vegetable broth
1 cup white wine
4 juniper berries, lightly crushed
2 bay leaves
6 stems thyme
6 carrots, cut in thick 3-inch sticks
1 1/2 pounds white or Savoy cabbage
8 slices lean bacon

Have each rabbit cut into 6 pieces (2 front legs, 2 back legs, and 2 pieces of the saddle). Use the rib cage for making stock or some other purpose as it is too bony for this dish. Season the rabbit with salt and white pepper, then dust with flour. In a large shallow braising dish, heat the olive oil and butter over medium heat. Put in the rabbit pieces a few at a time so the pan is not overcrowded and cook until golden on both sides, which takes about 6–7 minutes per side. Remove the pieces when they are done. Put in the garlic cloves and cook until they are slightly golden and a little soft. Add them to the rabbit pieces. Pour the stock and wine in the pan, add the juniper berries and let bubble until the liquid has reduced by a quarter. Season to taste with salt and pepper. Now replace the rabbit and garlic in the pan. Tuck the bay leaves, thyme, and carrot pieces in between the rabbit. Pull the large outer leaves from the cabbage and reserve. Cut the cabbage into 6–8 wedges and add these to the pan. Arrange the bacon on top, overlapping the slices a little and using as many as you need to cover the rabbit and the vegetables, the exact number therefore depending on the size and shape of your pan. Arrange the outer leaves of the cabbage on top, again covering the surface. These leaves and the bacon help keep the dish moist and flavorful. Put the lid on the pan, and simmer as slowly as possible over very low heat for 2 hours. Or start the pan on top of the stove, and transfer it to a 300-degree oven once it has started simmering. It's important to have a good seal to the pan so if the lid doesn't fit tightly cover the pan with a sheet of foil before putting the lid on. For serving, discard the outer leaves of the cabbage. Remove the rabbit and bacon to a serving dish and surround with the carrots and cabbage. Boil up the liquid in the pan and strain it over the rabbit and vegetables. Serves 4–6.

MALTESE CABBAGE WITH BACON

This easy recipe comes from Malta, a Mediterranean island poised between Libya and Italy. It was long ruled by Britain, and the bacon in this recipe is probably British in inspiration. But Malta also shares many dishes with its Italian neighbour, so you could substitute pancetta for the bacon.

6 slices bacon
8 cups shredded cabbage
Salt and freshly ground black pepper

Fry the bacon until the fat is golden. Cut it into 1-inch pieces. Discard all but 2 tablespoons of the fat. Drop the shredded cabbage into a large pan of boiling water with 1 teaspoon salt. Let it come back to the boil and boil steadily for 2–3 minutes. Drain the cabbage through a sieve, pressing to get out as much water as possible, Reheat the bacon fat, and stir the cabbage into it. Cook for a minute or two, stirring all the time so that any remaining water evaporates. Stir in the reserved bacon pieces and season with black pepper. (You probably won't need salt as the bacon is salty and the cabbage was cooked in salted water). Serves 4–6.

Carrots play a vital flavoring role in soups, stews, and casseroles because they work amiably with meats and other vegetables. They are so amiable in fact that, like old friends, they make no demands and can be easily taken for granted. But carrots can also be the leader of the band as in the recipes below. Most of our carrots are bright orange, but in their native countries of Afghanistan and India they are scarlet or crimson, and now these varieties are showing up on Valley farmstands. Look for yellow carrots too.

MEXICAN CARROT AND CUCUMBER STICKS

In Mexico bars often serve a plate of these sticks with a drink. They're perfect: exhilarating and with far fewer calories than nuts or cocktail kibble. If you see red or yellow carrots on a local farmstands, use them in this recipe alongside some of the regular orange carrots. Jazz the plate with a few black olives if you like.

4 carrots, peeled
2 small-medium pickling cucumbers or half an
 English cucumber, washed
Juice of 1–2 limes
Powdered dried hot chilis such as New Mexican or
 use chili powder
Salt to taste
Several torn leaves of cilantro

Quarter the carrots longways and cut them into sticks about 4 inches long. Leave the peel on the cucumbers. Halve them longways, cut each half into three and then, if necessary into sticks. Scatter the carrots and cucumbers on a plate. Squeeze the limes so you have a quarter cup of juice. Pour it over the vegetable sticks. Sprinkle with the powdered chili peppers or the chili powder and salt. Scatter the cilantro on top. Serves 6–8 with drinks.

MUSTARD MINT CARROTS

This recipe comes from Mary Ellen Warchol of Stockbridge Farm in Deerfield. Her husband John grows an enormous array of herbs and vegetables. They also grow lavender. Mary Ellen contrives wonderful recipes for using all these good things, which she demonstrates at local events and also at Pestopalooza, the August celebration of basil and other herbs at the farm. She notes that this simple recipe for carrots is best at room temperature, but if you prefer them cold they can be held in the fridge. For another of her recipes turn to the Stockbridge Farm No-Fry Eggplant on page 52.

2 pounds carrots, washed, peeled and cut into 1/2-inch diagonal slices
1/2 cup extra-virgin olive oil
2 tablespoons Dijon mustard
1 tablespoon honey
1/2 teaspoon freshly ground pepper
1/2 teaspoon kosher or sea salt
1/2 cup sherry vinegar
1/2 cup chopped spearmint

Cook the carrots in boiling water until they are tender. Drain. Stir together the oil, mustard, honey, pepper, salt, and vinegar and toss the carrots in this mixture while they are still hot. Set aside to cool to room temperature. Just before serving add the mint and toss everything together. Serves 8.

BRAISED CARROTS AND LEEKS

This easy yet elegant little dish is perfect for serving with fish and seafood. It's good also with chicken and lamb.

4 medium carrots, peeled
4 medium leeks, washed
1 tablespoon butter
Salt and white pepper
1/3 cup white wine
2 teaspoons chopped parsley or snipped chives

Cut both carrots and leeks into matchsticks about 2 inches long by 1/4 inch wide. Melt the butter in a small saucepan and add the carrots. Stir them around, sprinkle lightly with salt and pepper, then cover the pan and set it over a very low heat for 5 minutes or until the carrots have softened. Check once or twice to make sure the carrots aren't catching on the pan. Add the wine and turn up the heat so it bubbles for a minute. Add the leeks on top of the carrots, cover the pan again, and return to a low heat for 3–4 minutes. Stir the leeks into the carrots, and continue cooking with the lid on the pan for another 3–4 minutes or until both vegetables are tender. Stir in half the parsley or chives and adjust the pepper and salt to your taste. Serve garnished with the remaining parsley or chives. Serves 4.

CHOPPED CARROTS AND SWEDE

Britain has several regional dishes in which two or more vegetables are mashed together. Colcannon (see page 26) is an Irish example. This combination of carrots with rutabaga is from the North of England. What's a Swede got to do with this dish? Swede is the English name for rutabaga, so-called because the vegetable arrived from Sweden in the eighteenth century. To be good this combination should be chopped with a blunt knife so that you get a speckled mixture rather than a uniform purée. It needs a generous dose of pepper.

1 pound carrots (about 8 medium), washed and scraped
1 pound rutabaga (about a medium rutabaga) peeled
Salt to taste
1 tablespoon butter
Pepper to taste

Cut the carrots and rutabaga into one inch chunks. Put them in a saucepan cover plentifully with water, add half a teaspoon of salt, and boil for 20 minutes or until completely tender. Drain and return them to the hot pan. Using dinner knife rather than a sharp kitchen knife, chop the vegetables until they are thoroughly mixed but not mashed. The mixture should have orange and yellow speckles. Stir in the butter and season well with pepper and more salt if necessary. Serves 6 as a side dish.

CARROT AND MINT PILAF

Versions of this aromatic pilaf appear in many countries of the Middle East and in India. The spices vary, as do the proportions of rice and carrots: some version use whole carrots and only a couple of tablespoons of rice, while others are rice dishes with not much more than a carrot garnish. This version gives equal play to both ingredients. For extra drama, simmer 1/3 of a cup of wild rice in 1/2 cup lightly salted water for 50–55 minutes or until tender. Drain if necessary and fold into the pilaf a minute or two before serving.

> *3/4 cup basmati rice*
> *4 medium-large carrots (about 10–12 ounces)*
> *1 tablespoon butter*
> *1 tablespoon vegetable oil*
> *1 tablespoon chopped onion or shallot*
> *1 teaspoon cumin seeds*
> *Seeds from 2 cardamom pods, or substitute 2 cloves*
> *1 bay leaf*
> *1/2 teaspoon salt or to taste*
> *1 tablespoon chopped fresh mint or parsley*

Put the rice in a bowl and cover it plentifully with cold water. Set aside. Peel the carrots and cut them into matchsticks about one and half inches long. In a shallow pan, warm the butter and oil over low heat. Stir in the onion or shallot, and let it gently soften for 3–4 minutes. Stir in the cumin seeds and the cardamom seeds or cloves, then stir in the carrot matchsticks and cook for 2 minutes. Now drain the basmati rice and stir it in until it glistens with the oil and butter. Finally pour in 1 1/2 cups water, and add the bay leaf and salt. Increase the heat, and cook quite briskly until most of the water has been absorbed and the bubbles have left the surface pitted with holes. Cover the pan tightly, and cook on the lowest possible heat (or just let it sit on the turned-off burner) for about 5 minutes or until the rice and carrots are tender and all the water has been absorbed. Transfer to a heated serving bowl. Garnish with chopped mint, cilantro, or parsley. Serves 4–6.

CARROT AND PINEAPPLE CAKE

Carrot cake is a popular choice for special occasions like birthdays and Father's Day. This rich and fruity version entices with the tropical aromas of pineapple, cinnamon, coriander, and mace or nutmeg. You could serve it simply dusted with confectioner's sugar, or gild it with the cream-cheese frosting suggested below. If you are feeling very enterprising, you could even add marzipan carrots, made by coloring commercial marzipan or almond paste orange, then shaping it into mini-carrots. A feathery sprig of fennel or a little tuft of parsley can do for the leaves.

8-ounce can crushed pineapple
1 cup golden raisins
1/2 cup coarsely chopped walnuts
1 cup plus 2 teaspoons all-purpose flour
1 cup cake flour
1 teaspoon baking soda
2 teaspoons baking powder
1 tablespoon cinnamon
1 teaspoon powdered coriander
1/2 teaspoon powdered mace or nutmeg
4 eggs
1 1/4 cups canola oil or another bland vegetable oil
1 cup dark brown sugar
1/2 cup white sugar
1 teaspoon vanilla extract
1/2 pound (4 medium-large) carrots, grated

Cream Cheese Frosting:

6 tablespoons butter at room temperature

8-ounce package cream cheese at room temperature
2 cups confectioner's sugar
1–2 tablespoons reserved pineapple juice

Grease a 9-inch springform cake pan or another pan of the same capacity and line the base with baking parchment. Preheat the oven to 350 degrees.

Tip the crushed pineapple into a sieve set over a bowl and let the juice drain off while you prepare the other ingredients. Reserve the juice for the frosting. Combine the raisins and walnuts in a bowl with 2 teaspoons of all-purpose flour and toss lightly to coat them. In a large mixing bowl, mix thoroughly the cup of all-purpose flour with the cake flour, baking soda, baking powder, cinnamon, coriander, mace or nutmeg. In another bowl or the bowl of a food processor, put the eggs, oil, dark-brown sugar, white sugar, and vanilla extract. Whisk for 4 minutes or process for 2 minutes to thoroughly combine all these ingredients into a mixture that has the thickness of a pancake batter. If you rub a little between your fingers, it should not feel grainy with sugar.

Make a well in the center of the dry flour mixture, tip in about half the egg mixture and using a spatula, stir to fold the flour into the wet ingredients. When progress has been made, make another well and tip in the rest of the egg mixture. Continue folding until the two mixtures are entirely blended. Stir in the walnuts and raisins, adding them in 2 batches and stirring after each one. Finally, stir in the grated carrot and crushed pineapple. Pour the mixture into the prepared pan. With the end of a spatula or table knife draw a ring about 1 inch in from the edge of the pan so you leave a groove. This can prevent the cake rising into a pyramid, which makes it harder to frost. Bake for 50–60 minutes or until a toothpick or skewer poked in the center comes out clean. Remove the cake from the oven and let cool on a wire rack. After 20 minutes, run a knife between the pan and the cake, and then loosen the clasp on the pan. Remove the cake and sit it top side down on the rack so you can lift off the base of the pan and the parchment paper. Turn it the right way up and let cool completely before frosting.

To make the frosting, beat together the butter and cream cheese. Add a cup of confectioner's sugar and beat it in. Mix in 1 tablespoon of the reserved pineapple juice, then beat in the other cup of confectioner's sugar. Assess the thickness of the frosting, If necessary to make it spreadable, thin it with a little more juice, adding a few drops at a time so it doesn't get too sloppy. Spread on the cooled cake, starting with the sides and then going over the top. If you want a layer cake, make a double batch of frosting, then cut the cake in two or three transversely, and sandwich together the layers with frosting before going on to cover the sides and top. Serves 10-12.

Cauliflower is the most elegant member of the numerous cabbage family. Mark Twain derided it as "nothing but cabbage with a college education." If so, it was tuition money well-spent. Cauliflower is flavorful without being overwhelming, and its billowy shape looks inviting, especially when gently blanketed with a sauce. If you shop in farmers' markets and at farmstands, you will find local farmers proudly offering their cauliflowers, including, sometimes, the green romanesco kind, which grows in rambunctious whorls and pinnacles. Cook these like the white-headed cauliflowers. Cauliflower is one of the many vegetables that have a special affinity with cheese, as in the following two recipes. But as the recipe for Indian-Style Cauliflower with Potatoes shows, it's good in other ways too. The most important cooking tip is not to let it get soggy. Avoid this by poking the stalk with a skewer frequently when it's cooking. As soon as it's tender, drain it well before serving or mixing with other ingredients.

CLASSIC CAULIFLOWER CHEESE

A good case could be made that this is the most perfect – or at least one of the most perfect – of vegetable dishes. Unlike many vegetable dishes it can be made ahead and be reheated without spoiling. It's large enough to feed a crowd as a side dish, and nutritious enough to be a vegetarian main dish. Main thing, though, is that it tastes wonderful.

C | 37

Cauliflower cousins with a cabbage relative

1 large cauliflower, about 2 1/2–3 pounds
Salt to taste
3 tablespoons butter
4 tablespoons all-purpose flour
1 teaspoon dry mustard powder or pinch cayenne
1 1/2 cups milk
8 ounces grated extra-sharp Cheddar cheese (about 3 loosely packed cups)
2 tablespoons breadcrumbs made from day-old bread

Wash the cauliflower and cut off the surrounding leaves and some of the base of the stem. Cut the head of cauliflower into 6 pieces. Bring a large pan of water to the boil, add a teaspoon of salt and then the cauliflower pieces. Bring the water back to simmering and cook the cauliflower for 15–18 minutes or until a skewer slides into the thickest part of the stalk without meeting resistance. Remove the cauliflower from the water with a slotted spoon and let it drain in a colander. For the moment reserve the liquid.

To make the cheese sauce, melt the butter in a heavy sauce pan over low heat. Remove it from the heat and stir in the flour and mustard powder (or cayenne) to make a smooth but stiff paste. Loosen this by stirring in half a cup of the milk. Return it to the heat, and stirring all the while with a whisk, add another half cup of milk. As the lumps disappear, add the remaining milk and when the mixture is smooth and simmering stir in all except a couple of tablespoons of the grated cheese. When it has melted into the sauce, add half a cup of the reserved cooking liquid. Let the sauce simmer, stirring often until it has thickened. Taste for saltiness. If you think more salt is necessary, add it.

Preheat the oven to 350 degrees. Grease a casserole or other shallow baking dish with a little butter. Put in the drained cauliflower sprinkle it with half the reserved cheese over it. Pour on the sauce, making sure to let it trickle into the crevasses of the cauliflower and to cover all the top surfaces. Mix the remaining cheese and breadcrumbs and scatter on top. Bake for 15–20 minutes or until the sauce is bubbling and the crumb topping is golden brown. (If you prefer, you can prepare this as far as covering the cauliflower with the sauce, and finish baking it several hours later – or even next day. Keep it in the fridge if delaying the baking for more than 2 hours. In this case, cover with foil and bake for 30–35 minutes as it will need extra time to reach serving temperature). Serves 6–8 as a side dish.

CAULIFLOWER GRATIN WITH TOMATOES

This recipe is based on one that Irene Nelson of Amherst found in *Food Combining for Health: A New Look at the Hay System* by Doris Grant and Jean Joice (Thorsons, 1984). The Hay system was developed by a nineteenth-century American surgeon William Hay, who advocated a diet based on vegetables, fruits, whole grains, and unprocessed starches, with little meat. In its simplest form this recipe is simply cauliflower mashed with cottage cheese and cheddar. But it positively begs for variations. For example, lightly cooked vegetables such as peas or green beans could be added to the cauliflower mixture. For serving as a main dish Irene Nelson adds a couple of beaten eggs or several different cheeses. The version below has eggs for extra protein, a crisp topping of breadcrumbs to complement the creamy cauliflower, and a bright edging of tomato slices.

1 medium cauliflower (about 1 1/2–2 pounds)
1 cup low-fat cottage cheese
2 eggs, lightly beaten
4 ounces grated sharp Cheddar or other cheese
salt and pepper to taste
1/4 cup grated fresh breadcrumbs
1 tablespoon grated Parmesan
2 firm ripe tomatoes, cut in half-moon slices

Heat oven to 375 degrees and grease a shallow baking dish. Cut the cauliflower into 8 to 10 pieces including all but damaged parts of the stalk and any leaves. Put them in a pan with enough salted water to cover them. Simmer until tender then drain thoroughly, and mash with potato masher. Stir in the cottage cheese, eggs, and Cheddar. Taste for seasoning and add salt and pepper as needed. Turn the mixture into the prepared baking dish. (You can prepare ahead to this point if you like). Bake for 10 minutes, then remove from the oven and line the tomato slices around the edge of the dish. Mix the crumbs and Parmesan and sprinkle the mixture in the center. Return the dish to the oven and bake for another 15 minutes. Serves 4 as a vegetarian main dish; 6 as a side-dish.

INDIAN-STYLE CAULIFLOWER WITH POTATOES

Most Indian restaurants include a cauliflower dish on their menu. This is a typical example, and of course it would be good with Indian food. But it's good too with grilled or roast meats and vegetables.

1 pound potatoes, peeled and cut in bite-size pieces
Salt to taste
1 small-medium cauliflower
2 tablespoons butter
2 teaspoons cumin seeds
1 large onion, peeled and chopped
1 teaspoon powdered turmeric
2 teaspoons powdered coriander
1 tablespoon chopped fresh ginger
2–3 medium tomatoes, peeled seeded and chopped

*1 small jalapeño, finely chopped or pinch red-
    pepper flakes*
1 tablespoon coarsely chopped cilantro or parsley

Drop the potatoes into a pan of boiling water with 1/4 teaspoon salt, and boil for 6–8 minutes until slightly softened but not fully cooked. Discard the leaves and stalk of the cauliflower. Cut into bite-size florets. Drop these into a pan of water with 1/4 teaspoon salt and blanch for 3 minutes. Drain and reserve some of the cooking liquid.

Melt the butter in a sauté pan, stir in the cumin seeds and then the onion. Let it cook gently for 3–4 minutes, then stir in the turmeric and coriander followed by the tomatoes, ginger, and chopped jalapeno or red pepper flakes. Pour in half a cup of the reserved cauliflower liquid, then add the cauliflower and potatoes. Stir gently so the potatoes and cauliflower are coated with the spicy mixture. Simmer for 8–10 minutes. Check that the liquid doesn't evaporate. The vegetables should not be swimming in it, but the cauliflower and potatoes should be moist. If they are drying out, add more cauliflower liquid. Alternately you could add tomato juice or just plain water. Also check the seasoning and add salt if you think it necessary. Serves 6 as a side-dish.

Gnarly celeriac makes elegant soup

C

Celeriac, also called celery root, looks like a large pale turnip with a gnarly knot of roots. It's no beauty, but for versatility it's hard to beat. With a distinct flavour of celery it can be boiled and mashed like other root crops, either alone or mixed with potatoes or carrots or both. It can be grated and made into winter salads; it can add flavour to stews, and it makes delicious soup.

CELERIAC SOUP WITH SCALLOPS

You can serve this soup for lunch with just one scallop in the center; for supper you can serve it with a few more or with a mixture of scallops and shrimp, or even with a 4-ounce fillet of haddock or cod. It's also delicious on its own, simply garnished with chopped celery leaves and chives.

1 celeriac weighing 1 1/2–2 pounds, peeled and cut in chunks
1 medium onion, chopped
1 6-inch stalk celery, chopped
1 small clove garlic, chopped
1 bay leaf
4 black peppercorns
1/2 teaspoon salt or more to taste
1 cup half-and-half or whole milk
1 teaspoon butter or oil
Scallops (4 for lunch serving or 16 for supper)
1 tablespoon chopped celery leaves
2 teaspoons snipped chives

Put the celeriac chunks, onion, celery, garlic, bay leaf, peppercorns, and salt into a saucepan and add 4 cups of water or enough to cover the vegetables. Cover and bring to the boil. Simmer for 25 minutes or until the celeriac is tender. Drain off and reserve the liquid. Discard the bay leaf. Put the vegetables into a food processor and whizz them until smooth. Alternately simply mash them by hand. Return the vegetables to the pan. Also add the reserved cooking liquid and the half-and-half or milk. Bring to simmering point and taste. Add more salt if necessary, and more milk or water if you want the soup to be thinner.

Meanwhile, grease a frying pan with the butter or oil and heat it over high heat. Put the scallops in the pan in a single layer, reduce the heat and cook the scallops for 3 minutes on the first side and 2 minutes on the second side.

Serve the soup into shallow soup plates. Position the scallops in the center of each serving. Mix the chopped celery leaves with the chives and sprinkle some over each serving. Serves 4.

Corn is our most everywhere-and-any-time food. At breakfast in comes in basics such as cornflakes and corn muffins. At lunch and dinner it shows up in a chowder or soup or tacos. Then there are side-dishes of polenta, succotash, and cornbread plus snacks such as popcorn, corn chips, and tostitos. Add to this list the nearly invisible commercial uses of cornstarch and corn syrup and most of us consume corn in some form every single day. Few doubt, however, that the very best way to eat corn is to pick an ear from the stalk, shuck it, then drop it into a pan of boiling water. When it's this fresh it takes only a minute or two to cook, and all it needs is butter and salt to make it perfect. But as the ubiquity of corn in our diet shows, there are lots of recipes for corn. Here are a few winners.

GRILLED CORN

In Mediterranean countries vendors set up grills in parks and along sea fronts to cook corn. Soon its toasty aroma has enticed kids from the swings and couples from their tête-à-têtes, and everyone is nibbling the browned kernels from the cob. That same smell often reigns over local yards in corn season. Here are the basic instructions.

8 ears of corn or as needed
Sea salt
1 stick softened butter, or more as needed

Prepare a low charcoal fire in the barbecue grill or preheat a grill to 350 degrees. Pull back the husks from the corn and remove the strands of corn silk. Replace the husks so the kernels are covered. Place on the grill and cook for about 15 minutes or until the kernels are cooked. If you like, you can open the husks a few minutes ahead of time and char the kernels a little. Serve with soft butter to brush on top and salt. Sea salt is tastiest and if you have one of those fancy salts culled from salt flats this is a chance to use it. Maldon salt – from England but available in many local markets – is divine. Serves 4–8.

MARGARITA CORN SALSA

This recipe comes originally from Nikki Cieslik of Whately, who says she invented it to capture the flavors of her favorite drink. Her family grows numerous varieties of corn that she sells on her farmstand. It's on Route 5 in Deerfield, just north of Historic Deerfield and close to fields where the corn grows so it gets to her counter fresh, fresh, fresh. Like most local growers, the Ciesliks like to celebrate 4 July with their first harvest, but growing lots of varieties ensures that the farmstand has supplies well into the fall, Nikki Cieslik says that the corn aficionados among her customers especially look forward to the arrival of Silver Queen, a late-season variety.

>   *3 ripe tomatoes, peeled, seeded and chopped*
>   *1–3 jalapeño peppers,*
>   *1 green bell pepper, seeded and diced in 1/4-inch dice*
>   *1 small red onion, peeled and chopped*
>   *2 cups roasted or cooked corn kernels (from 2–3 ears of corn)*
>   *1/2 cup commercial margarita mix*
>   *Salt to taste*

As you chop the tomatoes put them into a colander or sieve set over a bowl to collect their juice. Use just one jalapeño for a medium-hot taste; more if you want a really fiery salsa. Chop them fine, discarding any seeds. Combine them with the green bell pepper, the onion, the corn kernels, and the tomatoes. Stir in the margarita mix and a little salt. Assess how much liquid you have. If you think you need more add some of the tomato juice that has collected in the bowl. Serve with corn chips. Enough for 8–10.

CORN LEEK AND SALMON CHOWDER

Packed with big flavors, this main-dish chowder looks rather elegant with its pretty pastel palette of pink, green, and yellows.

3 medium-large leeks, trimmed and washed
2 tablespoons butter
3 medium potatoes, peeled and cut into 1/2-inch cubes
Salt and white pepper
2 cups water or fish stock
Kernels from 2–3 ears of white or regular corn
3 cups milk
2 tablespoons snipped fresh chives or chopped parsley

Slice the leeks into 1/2-inch pieces. Discarding skin and bones, cut the salmon into bite-size pieces. In a large pan over moderate heat, melt the butter. Add the leeks. Stir in half the potatoes and season with salt and pepper. Add half the salmon, then the rest of the potatoes and then the remaining salmon, seasoning each layer as you go. Add 2 cups water, cover and simmer for 10 minutes. Add the corn kernels and the milk and simmer for 4–5 minutes, or until the potatoes are tender. Check the seasoning. Stir in 1 tablespoon of the chives. Ladle into soup bowls and garnish with the remaining chives. (Or replace the chives in whole or in part with parsley.) Serves 4–6.

CHICKEN WITH CORN AND CIDER

Cider combines with corn to make this an especially delicious supper dish. Using chicken thighs that have their bones intact adds extra flavor, but if you prefer you can use boneless ones.

2 tablespoons canola or other vegetable oil
1 medium onion, chopped
6 skinned chicken thighs, preferably bone in
Salt and white pepper to taste
1 1/2 cups cider

1 tablespoon chopped fresh tarragon or 1 teaspoon dried
2 tablespoons all-purpose flour
2 cups corn kernels, freshly shucked from 2–3 ears of corn.
1/2 cup light sour cream

Heat the oil in a frying pan over moderate heat. Add the chopped onion and cook until softened then remove from the pan with a slotted spoon. Add the chicken thighs to the pan and cook for 4–5 minutes, then turn them over and season with salt. Add 1 1/4 cups of the cider and the tarragon, and finally the reserved onion. Cover the pan and lower the heat so that the liquid is just simmering. Cook for 20 minutes. Remove the chicken from the pan.

Mix the flour with the remaining 1/4 cup cider so you have a thin paste. Add some of the hot liquid from the pan, and when it is mixed in stir the flour mixture into the pan along with the sour cream. Return the chicken pieces to the pan and bring simmer for 3–4 minutes, then add the corn kernels. Cover the pan again and continue cooking gently for 3 more minutes or until the corn is cooked.

Good with mashed potatoes or latkes. Serves 4–6.

Other recipes: Corn is one of the sunshine-yellow ingredients in The Shakers Heavenly Squash page 124. It teams with zucchini in Mexican Zucchini with Cream on page 140, and with potatoes in Twice-baked Potatoes with Tuna and Corn on page 103.

Cucumbers thrive in the flat fields around Hadley, and home gardeners find them an easy crop to grow. Like most vegetables, the local ones have bags more flavor than those trucked in from elsewhere. They are popular in salads, of course, and also in pickles. But cucumbers can also be cooked. This was the commonest way of using them in the eighteenth-century, but mostly we have forgotten about these older recipes. Simply peel and cut an English cucumber or two smaller ones into cubes discarding the seeds, then toss them in a pan with 2 tablespoons of melted butter, add about 3/4 cup stock or water plus herbs and seasonings to taste; cover the pan and simmer gently for about 12–15 minutes or until tender. For a more elaborate dish try the following recipe from Sri Lanka, which teams cooked cucumbers with shrimp.

FLOWER BY THE WAYSIDE CURRY OF CUCUMBER AND SHRIMP

This dish is based on a more complex recipe in *Culinary Jottings for Madras* by Colonel A. Kenney-Herbert, first published in 1907. The Colonel's *Jottings* told British residents of India how to instruct their Indian cooks in the making of British, French and even traditional Indian dishes. He called this curry a "flower by the wayside" because Sri Lanka – formerly called Ceylon – was the first stop on the subcontinent after the long voyage from England. Having described ship-board curries as "cuddy barbarisms – saffron-tinted swill covering sundry knotty lumps of potato and a few bony atoms of mutton," the Colonel praised Sri Lankan curries for their artful mingling of seafood or chicken with coconut milk, spices, and vegetables. They were, he said, "flowers by the wayside" to be enjoyed for their delicacy.

1 English cucumber about 12 inches, peeled
1 1/4 pounds large shrimp
3 tablespoons butter
1 medium onion, cut in half and thinly sliced
1 clove garlic, finely minced
1 tablespoon chopped fresh ginger
1 tablespoon all-purpose flour
2 teaspoons turmeric
1/2 teaspoon cloves
1/2 teaspoon cinnamon
pinch of dried hot pepper flakes
1 cup broth from cooking the shrimp or vegetable or chicken stock
1 can light coconut milk
Salt and white pepper to taste
1 teaspoon sugar (optional)

Cut the peeled cucumber into 4 longways and remove the seeds. Cut each long section into 1-inch pieces. Drop them in a pan of lightly salted water and cook for 10 minutes. Drain and set aside.

Remove the shells from the shrimp and set aside. Remove and discard the dark vein along the edge of the shrimp. Drop the shrimp into a pan of cold water and bring it to simmering point. When the shrimp have turned pink remove them from the pan immediately and drop them into a bowl of ice water. Add the reserved shells to the water you cooked the shrimp in and simmer for 5 minutes, then drain, reserving the liquid but discarding the shells.

Melt the butter in a shallow pan, and stir in the thinly sliced onion, minced garlic, and ginger. Cook gently over low heat and with a lid on the pan so the onions don't take any color. When they are tender stir in the flour, and then the turmeric, cloves, cinnamon, and pepper flakes plus half a cup of the water reserved from cooking the shrimp shells, and half the can of coconut milk. Stir until the mixture is smooth. Add the reserved shrimp and cucumber and the rest of the coconut milk. Cook gently over low heat to reheat the shrimp and cucumber. Taste and add salt and white pepper to taste. A little sugar – not more than a teaspoon – can be added too; it helps to bring the flavors together. Serves 4.

CUCUMBER SANDWICHES

Cucumber sandwiches taste so deliciously more than the sum of their parts that people who have never eaten one wonder why they are such an icon of English afternoon tea. Their charm is the unique combination of thin crustless bread with butter and slightly salty cucumbers. They taste divine. Refreshing too. This is one sandwich on which mayonnaise or margarine just cannot do the job.

1/2 cucumber, peeled and thinly sliced
salt
12 thin slices buttered white bread, crusts removed
white pepper

Put the thin slices of cucumber on a plate and sprinkle with salt. Leave for 20 minutes then rinse to get rid of excess salt and pat with paper towels to dry. Arrange even layers of cucumber slices on 6 bread slices; dust lightly with white pepper and top with the other bread slices. Cut the sandwiches into triangles or fingers. Serves 6–12.

DR. JOHNSON'S CUCUMBER PICKLE

When Dr. Samuel Johnson created his ground-breaking English dictionary in the middle of the eighteenth century, his commitment to objective definitions wavered when he came to cucumber. His description reads: "A cucumber should be well sliced, and dressed with pepper and vinegar, and then thrown out as good for nothing." This is exactly the way my mother and grandmother prepared cucumber – though they ignored the instruction to throw it out. I've also seen cucumber served this way in Bermuda. It's a kind of instant pickle, and if you enjoy vinegary condiments, you'll like it. Malt vinegar delivers the authentic punch; for something less rambunctious use half malt and half cider vinegar. Quantities can be adjusted to your needs, but the crucial thing is that the cucumber slices should not be merely sprinkled with vinegar. They should be lolling around in a vinegar bath.

1 cup thinly sliced peeled cucumber
Salt and white pepper
1 cup malt vinegar or half malt and half cider
　　vinegars

Put the sliced cucumber into a shallow dish. Season with salt and a liberal quantity of pepper. Pour on the vinegar. Voila! Serves 4 or more.

TZATZIKI

From the eastern shores of the Mediterranean all the way over the Arabian peninsula to India, people make a cooling relish by mixing yogurt or sour cream with cucumbers. In Greece it's flavored with mint, garlic, and white pepper and called *tzatziki*; a similar mixture is *cacik* in Turkey. It's usually served with the many small dishes called *mezedes* that appear before the main dish and is also essential with lamb. It appears on gyro sandwiches throughout the eastern Mediterranean. A similar relish called *raita* is an adjunct to bean dishes or a cooling contrast to fiery foods in India.

> *1/2 English cucumber, washed but unpeeled*
> *About 1 tablespoon salt*
> *1 cup Greek yogurt*
> *1 tablespoon olive oil*
> *1 clove garlic, peeled and minced*
> *Powdered white pepper to taste*
> *1-2 teaspoons chopped fresh mint (optional)*

Thinly slice the cucumber then cut across the slices to make strips 1/4-inch wide or less. Put them on a plate and sprinkle with salt. Leave for 20–30 minutes, then rinse to remove the salt and pat dry. The strips will now be limp. In medium bowl stir together the Greek yogurt, olive oil, and garlic. Stir in the cucumber strips, and season with white pepper and salt if needed. Stir in the mint if you are using it. Makes about 1 1/4 cups.

Other cucumber recipes: Mexican Carrot and Cucumber Sticks on page 30 is another way to serve cucumbers. They also play a part in Picalilli page 151.

Delicata squash, cut in half longways, turns into green-striped yellow boats just waiting for a cargo. It's sometimes called sweet potato squash because its flesh can be very sweet. The name delicata suggests something sophisticated, perfumed perhaps. The following recipe picks up this hint with tiny pasta, orange zest, and mysteriously aromatic coriander.

Stripey delicata squash is good for stuffing

DELICATA BOATS LADEN WITH ORANGE-CORIANDER ORZO

You can find orzo in supermarket pasta sections. It comes in a small box so it is often stocked on a lower shelf.

2 delicata squash, each 7–8 inches long and weighing 14–16 ounces
1 large orange
3/4 cup uncooked orzo
Salt to taste
1 tablespoon olive oil
3 tablespoons chopped shallots or onions
1 tablespoon butter
1 1/2 teaspoons powdered coriander
2 teaspoons chopped parsley
2 tablespoons toasted sliced almonds (see page ix)

Wash the delicata squash, cut in half longways, and remove the seeds and the fibres around them. Cut 2 slices from the middle of the orange and cut into half-moons. Using a zester remove the zest from the remaining orange.

Bake the delicata cut side down on a lightly greased pan or dish. This takes 25–30 minutes in a 375-degree oven or around 9 minutes in a microwave. Meanwhile, bring 2 quarts of water to the boil in a saucepan; add a teaspoon of salt and the orzo and cook it until al dente – which takes 6–7 minutes. Drain and reserve the orzo.

In a small frying pan heat the olive oil, and soften the shallots or onions in it for 3–4 minutes. Stir in the coriander and butter, and then the drained orzo. Stir in about half the orange zest and squeeze in about a tablespoon of juice from the orange. Taste and add more salt if needed. When the mixture is hot, stir in half the parsley and pile it into the delicata halves. Sprinkle with the remaining orange zest, the parsley and finally the toasted almonds. Garnish with the orange slices so people can add more juice if they like. Serves 4.

Other recipes: The Carrot and Mint Pilaf on page 33 can be served in Delicata boats, as could the Sage and Apple Stuffing in the acorn squash recipe on page 3.

Eggplant got their name because the earliest examples in America looked like eggs. Now that most of the eggplant we see are large and purple or sometimes sausage-shaped or stripey, their name seems perverse. But the people who bring their produce to farmers' markets love growing new things, including old things newly discovered, so you may spot white eggplant looking like giant pearls.

The Arabs brought eggplant to southern Italy and Spain when they ruled there during the Middle Ages. It's no surprise then to find that Mediterranean countries and the lands further east have a huge array of eggplant dishes. And perhaps no surprise to discover that when eggplants reached the north they were regarded with suspicion. Writing in his influential *Herball* in 1597 John Gerard advised his English compatriots "to content themselves with the meate and sauce of our owne country than with fruit and sauce eaten with such peril; for doubtlesse these... have a mischievous qualitie." His suspicions of the eggplant were not entirely unfounded. It belongs to the same family as the poisonous deadly nightshade. So do tomatoes and potatoes. Recognising this Gerard and many other Renaissance botanists were cautious about eating these vegetables. Eggplants and tomatoes were therefore grown as garden curiosities whose charm lay in their dramatic bulbous fruits. Thomas Jefferson is credited as being among the first people to grow eggplant in America, but it did not become popular until the late nineteenth century or later, when Italian immigrants arrived with their recipes.

In most European languages eggplants have a name that derives from the Arabic *al-badinjan*. This becomes *berenjena* in Spanish and *aubergine* in French. It's aubergine also in England, so if you have an English cookbook that calls for this ingredient, think eggplant.

STOCKBRIDGE FARM NO-FRY EGGPLANT

Many recipes for eggplant begin with the instruction to salt it for an hour. The reason for this is that some varieties of eggplant can have a bitter taste, which is removed by salting. Bitterness is not a problem with Valley eggplant, but salting also has the effect of collapsing the cells of the vegetable, so it guzzles less oil when it is fried. Even so, eggplant can suck up quite a lot, thus loading itself with calories. Mary Ellen Warchol of Stockbridge Farm in Deerfield prevents this by baking her eggplant. She serves it as a side dish straight from the oven or layers it with the marinara sauce she makes from the tomatoes her husband grows. Another benefit of her method is that the slices can be frozen. She puts cooked slices on a sheet pan and slips it into the freezer. When they're frozen she packs them in freezer bags for storage. This way she can enjoy one of summer's heat-loving crops even in the depths of winter. Her recipe follows.

2 large purple eggplant, freshly picked if possible
1 cup wheat germ
3/4 cup grated Parmesan cheese
2 eggs
1/2 teaspoon freshly ground pepper
1 tablespoon chopped parsley or basil

Preheat the oven to 350 degrees, and lightly coat a baking sheet with cooking spray. Peel the eggplant if desired and slice into 3/4 inch rounds. Place the wheat germ, Parmesan cheese, pepper and herbs into a shallow bowl and mix them well. In another bowl mix the eggs with a tablespoon of water. Dip each eggplant slice into this egg mixture, then into the wheat-germ mixture. Place on the prepared baking sheet. When it's full bake for 10 minutes. Turn the slices over and bake for another 10 minutes or until the tip of a paring knife meets no resistance when it's inserted into the middle and the coating is light brown. Serves 6–8.

CAPONATA

Caponata is a Sicilian dish, a little like ratatouille but distinctive in its use of celery, olives, vinegar, pine nuts, and raisins. These last two ingredients along with the eggplant itself and the sweet-sour flavor of this dish reveal its Arabic roots. In Sicily and Italy caponata is eaten at room temperature, but on a cool New England evening it is delicious warm served alongside chicken or fish.

1 1/2–2 pounds eggplant, washed but unpeeled
Salt to taste
2–3 tablespoons golden raisins
About 1/2 cup olive oil
2 cups celery stalks cut in 1-inch pieces
1 large onion, chopped
2 cups chopped peeled fresh or canned tomatoes
1/2 cup wine vinegar
1 tablespoon sugar
1 small hot pepper, chopped or pinch of red pepper flakes
2–3 basil leaves, torn in bits
1 dozen or more to taste green olives
2 teaspoons capers
1–2 tablespoons toasted pine-nuts (see page v)

Cut the eggplant into 1/2-inch cubes. Put them in a colander sprinkling them liberally with salt as you go. Put the colander in the sink with a plate on top of the eggplant pieces to weigh them down. Let drain for an hour or longer, then rinse and dry them. Put the raisins in a small bowl and cover them with warm water. Set them aside.

Put half a cup of olive oil into a large frying pan and fry the eggplants until they are golden brown. Remove them onto paper towels to drain. In the same oil – or in some extra oil if necessary – fry the celery for 5 minutes. Drain it on paper towels. Add the chopped onion to pan, and cook until it has softened then add the tomatoes, vinegar, sugar, hot pepper, and basil leaves, and cook for about 15 minutes or until they have softened into a sauce. Return the eggplant and celery to the sauce and cook in it for just five minutes. Taste for seasoning and add salt if you would like. You can also adjust the sweet-sour balance by adding more vinegar or sugar; however, caponata should be more tart than sweet. Finally, off the heat stir in half the olives, half the capers, and half the pine nuts. Mound onto a serving dish and let cool to room temperature. Scatter the remaining olives, capers, and pine nuts on before serving. You can serve this with tuna or swordfish as a main dish, or garnished with anchovies or roasted red pepper strips as an appetizer, or eat it with chunky bread for lunch. Serves 4 or more.

EGGPLANT AND LAMB CASSEROLE

The amounts of eggplant and lamb can be varied. Indeed, this stew, with its flavors of eastern spice markets, could be made vegetarian by omitting the lamb and stirring in a couple of cups of cooked chickpeas during the last 10 minutes.

2 pounds eggplant (about 2 largish ones)
Salt as needed
2–4 tablespoons olive oil
1 1/2 pounds boneless lamb stew meat
1 large onion, chopped
2 cloves garlic, minced
6 basil leaves, torn
2 teaspoons powdered cumin or more to taste
1 teaspoon powdered coriander
4 large tomatoes, skinned and chopped
2 bay leaves
2 teaspoons chopped mint plus leaves for garnish

Cut the eggplant into slices. Cut these across these in both directions to make cubes. Put them in a colander and sprinkle well with salt. Leave for an hour or longer, then rinse and dry. Heat 2 tablespoon of the oil in a heavy pan, and sauté the chopped onion for about 5 minutes or until it has softened. Now add the meat and cook until the meat is brown on all sides. Remove from the pan and sprinkle it with the garlic, basil, cumin, and coriander, and season with a little salt. Add the eggplant cubes to the pan and cook them, adding more oil as needed. Cover but stir gently from time to time. After 10 minutes return the meat to the pan along with the chopped tomatoes, bay leaves, and the chopped mint. Cover again and simmer on the lowest heat for at least an hour. If it seems to be drying out, add more tomatoes or a little water. Serve garnished with mint. Serves 6.

EGGPLANTS WITH FETA AND BAY LEAVES

This recipe is inspired by one in Rosemary Barron's *Flavours of Greece* (Penguin Books, 1994). Choose the shapeliest bay leaves that you can find because they garnish as well as flavor the dish.

4 eggplants, each about 12 ounces
about 2 tablespoons salt
about 1/2 cup olive oil
white pepper to taste
1 pound feta cheese, cut in 8 slices
2 cups tomato sauce
2 teaspoons dried oregano
1 teaspoon powdered allspice
9 bay leaves
2 tablespoons grated Parmesan
2–3 tablespoons coarsely chopped flat-leaf parsley
  or torn basil leaves

Trim the stem end from the eggplants then cut them in half lengthways. Make some criss-cross slashes in the surface then sprinkle with the salt. Let them sit cut side down on a rack in the sink for 45–60 minutes. The salt will draw out liquid. Rinse this off and pat dry with paper towels. Heat about 1/4 cup of olive oil in in a large frying pan and place in cut side down as many eggplant halves as you can fit. Fry over moderate heat for 8–10 minutes or until they are golden. When they are done put them in a shallow baking dish such as a lasagne pan. Add more oil to the frying pan as needed and fry all the eggplant halves – cut side only – in the same way. Dust the eggplants with white pepper and put a feta slice on each eggplant half. (It doesn't need to cover the whole surface.)

Turn the oven to 350 degrees. In a saucepan over medium heat mix the tomato sauce with the oregano, allspice, and just one of the bay leaves. Let it simmer for 5 minutes. Spoon the sauce over the feta-topped eggplant, making sure to cover the cheese. Sprinkle lightly with the Parmesan then top each one with a bay leaf. Bake for 30–40 minutes, or until the eggplants are very tender. Check every now and then and add a little water to the dish if the sauce is drying up. Serve warm or at room temperature scattered with the parsley or basil. Serves 4–8.

F

Fennel looks slightly like celery. It's a mass of pale green and whitish stems, but while celery stems are separate, fennel stalks are packed together in a tight bulbous end, and instead of the leafy tops of celery, fennel has hollow rod-like stems feathered with emerald fronds. Despite its resemblance to celery, fennel belongs to the carrot family. Like carrots, it's well worth adding to soups and stews. But what gives fennel real distinction is its anise flavor, which makes it especially delicious with fish and seafood. In Italy, where it is a native plant, it is also eaten raw in salads or tossed in oil and butter and served with pasta. Thomas Jefferson wrote that "Fennel beyond every other vegetable is delicious." At the end of a meal he preferred eating fennel to fruit. Don't chuck the tubular stems: they are too stringy to eat but you can use them to flavor stocks or sit fillets of fish on them for baking. Use the fronds too: treat them as an herb for flavoring or for scattering as a pretty garnish.

Fennel with Pasta Seafood and Saffron Cream

FENNEL WITH PASTA SEAFOOD AND SAFFRON CREAM

In this recipe the fennel is cooked right in the pan with the pasta so the pasta picks up its anise flavor. You therefore need to choose small pasta shapes that need only 6–7 minutes to cook.

Be sure to soak the saffron for at least two hours, preferably more, to extract color and flavor. Saffron is the world's most expensive spice so you want to be able to savor its heady honey flavor in this luxurious confection of seafood and fennel. It's not a difficult dish to make, but it's important to work on its constituent parts before starting the cooking because it goes quickly at the end.

2 tablespoons warm milk
1 envelope powdered saffron or 1 very large pinch saffron threads
2 bulbs fennel weighing 1 1/2 pounds in total
3/4 cup cream
1 teaspoon fennel seeds
1 teaspoon salt plus more to taste
12 ounces small pasta such as sea-shells or pipette
1 pound large shrimp
16–20 large sea scallops
1 tablespoon butter
White pepper to taste

Stir the milk and saffron in a small bowl and set aside for a couple of hours (longer is good), stirring it from time to time to release the color and flavor. Cut the tubular stems and fronds off the fennel bulb and reserve them. Run a potato peeler over the outside of the fennel bulb to take off damaged or darkened bits. Slice the bulb downwards into quarter-inch slices, then cut these longways into quarter-inch strips, which will be about 2–3 inches long. Cut the fronds from the fennel stems; reserve a few sprigs for garnish and chop the remainder. Shell the shrimp, and using the sharp point of a knife, strip out the black vein. Rinse them, put them in a pan, and add water to cover them by an inch. Lightly grease a heavy frying pan with butter.

Put 3 quarts of water, a teaspoon of salt and the tubular fennel stalks in a pasta pan and bring to a boil. Simmer the fennel stalks for 5–10 minutes to flavor the water, then discard them. Let the water come to a rolling boil and add the fennel strips and the pasta. Cook until al dente – about 6 minutes. As soon as you put the pasta in the pan, mix the cream and the fennel seeds with the saffron and its milk. Also put the pan of shrimps on the heat, add 1/4 teaspoon salt, bring to boiling and simmer for 2–3 minutes or until they have become pinkly opaque. At the same time heat the greased frying pan over high heat, and when hot place the scallops in it. Let them cook for 3 minutes or until they are brown on one side and flip to brown the other side. The pasta and fennel, the shrimp, and the scallops should all be cooked at about the same time.

Drain the pasta and fennel and the shrimp. Return the pasta pan to low heat, add the butter and let it melt. Now return the pasta and fennel to the pan and stir it around in the butter for a few seconds, then stir in the saffron mixture, shrimp, scallops, and a couple of teaspoons chopped fennel frond. Taste and add more salt or chopped fennel frond if you want, and white pepper to taste. Serve in individual dishes, garnished with fennel fronds. Serves 4–6.

BRAISED FENNEL WITH MUSSELS TOMATOES AND ROSEMARY

1 or 2 bulbs fennel, total weight 1 1/2 pounds
2 tablespoons olive oil
1 medium onion, peeled and chopped
2 cloves of garlic, peeled and minced
3 medium-large ripe tomatoes, peeled, seeded and coarsely chopped
1 teaspoon chopped fresh rosemary leaves
Salt to taste
2 pounds mussels, thoroughly washed
1 cup white wine
2 rosemary sprigs, each about 2 inches

Cut off the fennel's tubular stalks and fronds and reserve them. Pare away any browned or damaged parts of the bulb. Stand the fennel on the root end and cut in half from top to bottom. Lay the halves cut side down, and slice 1/4-inch thick. Cut the slices in half. Chop enough of the fennel fronds so that you have at least a teaspoonful chopped.

Heat the oil in a deep sauté pan or saucepan, add the chopped onion and cook for 2–3 minutes to soften it a little. Add the garlic, cook another minute, and then add the fennel. Stir everything together for a minute or two then stir in the chopped tomatoes, chopped fennel fronds, and chopped rosemary. Season with salt to taste. Cover the pan, and simmer for about 4–5 minutes or until the fennel strips have partly softened. Put the mussels on top, discarding any that are open or have broken shells. Stick in the rosemary sprigs and pour on the wine. Let it bubble, then cover and cook for 4 minutes or just until the mussels have opened. Serve from the cooking vessel garnished with the rosemary sprigs and more chopped fennel fronds and crusty bread or rice on the side. You can use the reserved fennel stalks and any leftover fronds for flavoring soups or fish. Serves 4.

Fiddleheads are fern shoots, so called because they thrust up in early spring looking exactly like the scroll of a violin. They are not any old fern shoots, but those of the ostrich fern (*Matteuccia struthiopteris*) that grow on the banks of the Connecticut River and in other moist places. Just as fiddleheads are coming through on the bank, shad, the largest member of the herring family, swim up the river from the sea, striving to reach their spawning grounds high up in the river. No surprise then that shad with fiddleheads is a traditional spring dish all along the Connecticut. Foragers gather fiddleheads for some local markets. Look for them in May. Better yet, befriend a forager who will show you the right kind of fern and where to gather them. Fiddleheads have a springtime taste that has something of asparagus in it and something of spinach. Their pretty coiled shape makes them a stunning companion to any main dish.

FIDDLEHEADS

1 pound fiddleheads
Salt to taste
Butter or extra-virgin olive oil to taste
Snipped chives, chive blossom petals, or chopped mint or parsley (optional)

Fiddleheads usually have traces of the brownish skin that covers them in the early stages of their growth. Soak them for 20 minutes or longer to loosen this skin, and remove it because it can taste bitter. Also trim off the dry end where they were cut from the stalk Bring a pan of lightly salted water to the boil, and drop the fiddleheads in it. Simmer them for 1 minute. If any remaining brown bits float to the surface, remove them. Discard the water. Bring a second pan of salted water to the boil, and cook the fiddleheads until tender, which takes about 3-4 minutes. Toss with butter or oil, and herbs if you like. Serves 6 as a side dish.

Other recipes: Fiddleheads can replace sugar-snap peas in Risotto with Sugarsnap Peas and Spring Herbs (page 90) or asparagus in Asparagus with Chiveblossom Vinaigrette (page 7).

Fiddleheads with shad are a springtime tradition

Green beans left on their plant would dry out and the little beans in the pod would become dry beans. For many centuries dry beans are just what people wanted because they are nutritious and easily stored over winter. Archaeologists have identified 8,000-year old beans in Peru, and when the first European settlers arrived in the Americas they found varieties and colors of beans far outnumbering those they knew in their homelands. But though America is the botanical home of many varieties of bean, green beans were not grown here as a commercial crop until the nineteenth century because the high proportion of pod to bean was not valued by people interested in stashing stuff for winter. Today, gardeners can choose varieties ranging from the elegantly thin *haricots verts* available in farmers' markets, to the common round bush beans and wax beans, and the flat-podded Italian beans and the runner beans that climb up poles. Green beans have lots of flavor buddies. Bacon is a stellar one. You can toss them with bacon pieces and a little bacon fat, or better yet, make an easy summer supper of new potatoes, green beans, and fried bacon. Almonds are another partner. Simply brown a couple of tablespoons of flaked almonds in butter then pour them, butter and all, on the beans. Toasted pine nuts also set off beans deliciously. For fewer calories, season beans with powdered cumin or toss them with cumin seeds at serving time. Green beans taste better tender rather than crisp; don't overcook them, but do let them simmer for a full 10 minutes.

GREEN BEANS WITH OLIVE OIL AND TOMATOES

The Greeks have a group of dishes called "oil dishes" because they require quantities of olive oil. Traditionally the oil made them luxurious because it was expensive and appreciated for its flavor rather than just as a cooking medium. Paradoxically, these rich oil dishes are suitable for the many fasting days in the Greek Orthodox calendar when animal products are forbidden. Oil dishes are also served as appetizers. Green Beans with Tomatoes is a favorite. Like much of Greek food, it's eaten at room temperature with bread, though it's equally good as a side dish.

1/2 cup olive oil (or more to taste)
1 medium onion, peeled, quartered and thinly sliced
1–2 cloves garlic, peeled and thinly sliced
1 1/2 pounds green beans, trimmed and cut into 2-inch lengths
Salt and pepper to taste
1 bay leaf
3 large ripe tomatoes, peeled, seeded and coarsely chopped
1/2 teaspoon powdered cumin
2 teaspoons oregano
2 tablespoons chopped parsley

Pour half the oil into a saucepan over low heat. Add the sliced onions and garlic, cover the pan and cook gently for 6–7 minutes so the onions soften without taking color. Stir in the green beans seasoned with a little salt and pepper. Add the bay leaf and the rest of the oil, cover and cook gently for a 5–7 minutes or until the beans have softened. Put the tomatoes on top. Cover the pan and continue cooking gently for 10 more minutes. Stir everything together and add the cumin, oregano and half the parsley. Cover and simmer slowly for 30 minutes or until all the vegetables have collapsed into a succulent mass. From time to time, check to make sure they are not sticking to the pan, adding more oil or a little water to prevent this. Transfer to a serving dish, and scatter the rest of the parsley on top. Serves 6 as a side dish.

ITALIAN GREEN BEAN SALAD

Years ago, I was invited to lunch by an elderly Italian lady who had only recently emigrated to America. As I entered her house she was tipping more green beans than I had ever seen into what looked like the world's biggest colander. I assumed she was planning to can them. In the sitting room we practiced a few English phrases and drank Riunite red wine with her husband. Time passed. I could smell nothing cooking. Then my hostess went into the kitchen and returned with the beans mounded on a giant oval platter, a basket of bread, and a carafe of olive oil. The beans were lunch. We ate them with the Riunite. They were divine. When we had finished, the husband, who spoke no English and therefore could not take no for an answer, made everyone a glass of Alka Seltzer. Part of the feast? Who knows, but it made a memorable ending.

> *1 pound (or more) flat Italian green beans*
> *Salt to taste*
> *2-3 tablespoons olive oil*
> *1-2 teaspoons white-wine or vinegar or lemon juice*
> *1/2 teaspoon dried oregano or more to taste*
> *1 tablespoon chopped flat-leaf parsley plus extra sprigs*

Trim the ends of the beans and cut them into 3/4-inch pieces. Bring a quart of water to a rolling boil, add 1/2 teaspoon of salt, then drop the beans in it. Cook for 8–10 minutes or until just tender. Drain, tip into a salad bowl, and let them cool off for 5–10 minutes. In another bowl mix the olive oil, vinegar or lemon juice, dried oregano, and about half the parsley. While the beans are still a little warm, pour this dressing on them and toss. Taste and add more salt if needed. Sprinkle with the rest of the chopped parsley and garnish with parsley sprigs. Serves 4.

GREEN BEAN CHUTNEY

This unusual chutney is good with meat or with Indian food. It should have a lot more beans than summer squash: about 80 percent beans to 20 percent squash, but the proportions don't have to be exact; you could use all beans if you like. For a hot condiment add a chopped jalapeño or a pinch of dried red pepper flakes.

1 pound green beans, trimmed
1 medium onion, chopped
1 teaspoon salt
1 medium summer squash
1 small jalapeño pepper, chopped or pinch red
  pepper flakes (optional)
1 1/2 cups white vinegar
3/4 cup white sugar
2 tablespoons corn starch
2 tablespoons mild or medium curry powder
1 medium-large carrot, peeled and grated

Cut the green beans into half-inch pieces. Put them in a pan with the chopped onions and salt and pour on enough boiling water to cover. Simmer for 10 minutes or until they have softened. Cut the squash into half-inch cubes and add them to the beans. If you want this to be a hot chutney, also add the jalapeno or red pepper flakes. Simmer for another 3–5 minutes, then drain.

In another pan mix the vinegar and sugar and bring to simmering point. In a small bowl stir the cornstarch into a thin paste with a tablespoon or two of cold water. Stir in a little of the hot vinegar, then stir the mixture into the vinegar pan. Bring to the boil and stir until it thickens. Stir in the curry powder, then the drained bean mixture, and finally the grated carrot. Simmer, stirring often for 4–5 minutes. Let cool then pour into sterilized jars (see page xii for sterilizing directions). This chutney has a lot of vinegar and sugar, which are preservatives, so there's no need to process in a boiling water bath. Store closed in a cool place and eat within 2 months. Makes about 2 1/2 pints.

Jeruslem artichokes are among the odder vegetables. They have nothing to do with Jerusalem, and they are not artichokes but the underground tubers of a kind of sunflower (*Helianthus tuberosus*). The flowers are about the size of a Shasta daisy, and they appear in September and early October, nodding on top of stalks that can be as tall as 6 or 7 feet. Only in November, when the flowers have long disappeared, can the tubers be dug up. They look rather like ginger roots or small knobbly potatoes. Their lumps and bumps make peeling tricky. It's best to wash them thoroughly, boil them in the skin for about 15 minutes or until tender, and then you can easily scrape the peel away. Eat them in chunks or mashed. When fresh they can also be eaten raw, and they make an excellent soup.

Jerusalem artichokes are North American natives. The first European to describe them was the French explorer, Samuel Champlain, who in 1605 discovered the indigenous Nauset people growing them right here in Massachusetts on Cape Cod. Champlain, who later colonized Québec and gave his name to New England's largest lake, described them as "roots with the taste of artichokes." This is true, especially when they are fresh from the

Knobbly Jerusalem Artichokes are Massachusetts natives

ground. But what about the epithet "Jerusalem?" The vegetable has nothing to do with the city, but when they reached Europe they became popular with the artichoke-loving Italians, who noticed the plant was a sunflower and called it *girasole,* which describes the sunflower habit of turning to the sun. In English this *girasole* became Jerusalem. From this we get two new terms. One is Palestine soup, a nineteenth-century Jerusalem artichoke soup so-called because the city of Jerusalem was then in Palestine. The other word is "sunchoke," which refers back to the sunflower origins, and was coined by Californian growers marketing the knobby tubers as a novelty in the 1980s.

Look for Jerusalem artichokes in November and December. Mostly they are pale-brown skinned with creamy-white flesh, but sometimes they are pinkish-purplish. They are still unfamiliar to many people, so they are often pricey (and always so in supermarkets). But since they are New England natives, they grow easily, reappearing year after year, so growing your own is an inexpensive option. You may also find them growing wild.

PALESTINE SOUP

This recipe is adapted from Eliza Acton's *Modern Cookery,* published in 1845. For good reason culinary historians regard this as the best English cookery book of the nineteenth century. She recommends veal stock, but notes that "where economy is a consideration, excellent mutton-broth, made the day before and perfectly cleared from fat, will answer very well." Most of us are unlikely to have either, but chicken or turkey stock or vegetable broth also answer very well.

> *1 pound Jerusalem artichokes*
> *2 tablespoon butter*
> *1/2 cup chopped onion*
> *1/2 cup chopped celery*
> *2 tablespoons chopped parsley*
> *Salt to taste*
> *1 quart chicken or vegetable or other stock*
> *1 cup cream or half-and-half*
> *Pinch cayenne pepper (optional)*

Wash the Jerusalem artichokes and drop them into a pan of cold water. Bring to the boil and simmer for 10 minutes. Drain and run cold water over the artichokes. The peel will now be loosened so remove it. Slice the vegetables.

In a saucepan, melt the butter and stir the artichokes and onion into it. Cover the pan and cook over very low heat for 5 minutes. Now add the celery, a tablespoon of the parsley, a pinch of salt and half the stock. Bring to the boil and simmer for about 10 minutes or until the vegetables are soft. Puree the mixture using either a blender, food processor, food mill or a sieve.

Return the puree to the pan and add the remaining stock and the cream, simmer for a couple of minutes then taste. Add salt if needed and the cayenne if you like it. Serve garnished with the rest of the parsley. Serves 4–6.

MOROCCAN-STYLE CHICKEN WITH JERUSALEM ARTICHOKES

In Morocco artichoke hearts would be used in dishes such as this but those who grow Jerusalem artichokes will find they work deliciously.

3/4 pound Jerusalem artichokes, scraped and cut in walnut-size pieces
Juice 1 lemon
2 tablespoons olive oil
2 onions, grated
2–3 cloves garlic, finely chopped
1 teaspoon powdered ginger
1/2 teaspoon powdered cumin
1/4 teaspoon turmeric
4 large bone-in chicken thighs
Salt to taste
Freshly ground black pepper
6 tablespoons chopped flat-leaf parsley
3 tablespoons chopped cilantro
1 preserved lemon
12–16 green or purple olives

Peel as much skin as possible from the Jerusalem artichokes, dropping them into a bowl of water with a few drops of lemon juice to prevent them browning.

In a pan which will hold the chicken pieces in one layer, heat the olive oil over moderate heat. Stir in the grated onion and garlic, and let them cook gently for 3–4 minutes. Stir in the ginger, cumin, and turmeric. Put in the chicken skin side down and season it with salt and a generous amount of freshly grated black pepper. Cook gently for about 5 minutes, then turn the chicken over, sprinkle with about half the parsley and cilantro, add a cup of water, cover the pan and cook gently for 20 minutes. Tuck the Jerusalem artichoke pieces around and under the chicken and cook for another 10–15 minutes. Finally, add the lemon juice, olives and the preserved lemon cut into strips. Cook gently for another 5 minutes to heat the olives and lemon through. Serve garnished with the rest of the parsley and cilantro.

Cous cous would be the typical accompaniment in Morocco, but rice or spaghetti squash are also good with this dish. Serves 4.

Kale is a kind of cabbage whose characteristic is that it doesn't form a head, instead it makes a bunch of showy green or bluish leaves with crinkly edges. It's a weather warrior, standing up to frost and even sprouting anew in spring when the winter has not been too severe. This means you can sometimes find it as soon as the farmers' markets get going in May, but really it's a fall crop. It makes a good side dish with beef and lamb. Some people like it in salads too, and it's a winner in soups.

PORTUGUESE KALE SOUP

Controversies rage around kale soup, called *caldo verde*, "green soup" in Portuguese. Should the sausages be cooked in the same pot as the vegetables? Or should they be done separately, as in this rather purist version of a classic dish — a favorite in both its European homeland and among the Valley's Portuguese community? You can do it either way, confident that with kale, potatoes, and sausage, you have here a complete meal rather than a first course soup.

> 5 medium-large potatoes, peeled and sliced
> 1 teaspoon salt
> 1 large onion, chopped
> 2 cloves garlic, chopped
> 4–6 tablespoons olive oil
> about 6 cups fresh kale, washed, trimmed and cut
>   into inch-wide strips
> 1 pound linguiça
> 1/2 pound chouriço or chorizo

Put the sliced potatoes, salt, onion, garlic and a tablespoon of olive oil in a large pot with 2 quarts water. Bring to the boil and cook for about 15 minutes. Remove from the heat and break up the potatoes – still in the liquid – with a potato masher so they are in biggish pieces. Add the strips of kale to the pan and return to the heat. Boil for another 8–10 minutes or until both potatoes and kale are tender. Meanwhile, prick the linguiça and chouriça and cut into 2-inch pieces. Heat a couple of tablespoons of olive oil in a large frying pan and fry the sausage in it for 10 minutes. Put a piece of each sort of sausage into each of 4 large soup bowls. Ladle the soup on top. Drizzle in a little of the remaining oil. Have more oil and either Portuguese or Italian bread on the side. Or have corn bread – the typical choice in much of Portugal.

Other recipes: You can use kale instead of cabbage in Colcannon on page 26 or instead of chard in the recipe for Pork and Chard Meatballs on page 130.

L | 71

Leeks and daffodils are the national symbols of Wales. They recall a battle against the Saxons in 640, when King Cadwallader's Welsh soldiers identified themselves by sticking leeks in their caps. Or perhaps it was daffodil leaves, which have the same spear-like shape. Today, leeks or daffodils appear on lapels on March 1, the day that the Welsh honor their patron saint, St. David. In Welsh cooking, leeks are essential in the *cawl,* the national stew of beef or lamb with autumn vegetables. In other dishes they sometimes take the place of onions because they grow better in the chill of this mountainous land. Here in the Valley too, it's possible to leave leeks in the ground and harvest them in spring. They are milder than onions and a favorite in soups, stews, pies, and tarts throughout Europe. The only two tricks to cooking them are first, to slit them and hold them under running water to rinse out the soil often trapped in their many layers, and then second, to cook them until they are tender, but don't overcook them because then they get slithery.

ANGLESEY EGGS

More and more often you see roadside signs for fresh eggs, and the vegetable growers who sell their crops in farmers' markets often bring eggs too. Their yolks are much more yellowy and their taste so much richer than mass-produced eggs. Use them in this supper dish – *Wyau Inys Mon* in Welsh – which comes from the island of Anglesey in North Wales.

> 1 1/2 pounds potatoes (about 3 large)
> Salt to taste
> 1 pound leeks (about 4 medium)
> 1–2 tablespoons butter
> 4 hardboiled eggs
> Cheese sauce made with extra-sharp Cheddar (see p. xi)
> 2 tablespoons grated extra-sharp Cheddar

Peel the potatoes, cut into chunks, and boil then in water with 1/2 teaspoon of salt for 20 minutes or until they are tender. Drain them. Mash them with a tablespoon of the butter.

Meanwhile, preheat the oven to 350 degrees and clean the leeks by removing all the dark-green top and the coarse outer leaves. Slit the leeks for about 6 inches downward, and splay the layers under a tap of cold running water to remove any soil collected there. Cut the white and tender green parts into half-inch discs. Cover with water, add a pinch of salt, simmer for about 10 minutes or until they are tender. Drain them and reserve the liquid. Stir the leeks into the mashed potatoes, and then beat well so that the mixture looks pale green. If this mash is stiff, add a little of the reserved leek liquid to make it softer and smoother, Spread this mixture in a greased shallow baking dish. Halve or quarter the hard-boiled eggs and settle them on top of the potato-leek mixture. Pour the cheese sauce over the eggs, and sprinkle with the grated cheese. Bake for 15–18 minutes or until the top is bubbly and splotched with brown patches. Serves 4.

LEEK-FILLED YORKSHIRE PUDDING

Made from an enriched Yorkshire pudding batter filled with leeks, this dish can be served as a side with meat – just like regular Yorkshire pudding – or for vegetarians it can be served with beans. It's also good with scrambled eggs or smoked salmon for brunch.

3–4 large leeks, cleaned and with outer leaves discarded
3 tablespoons butter
Salt to taste
3 eggs lightly beaten
1 1/2 cups milk
1 cup flour
2 teaspoons sugar

Discard all the coarse and dark green leaves at the top and on the outside of the leeks. Wash the leeks by making 6-inch slits from the top down so you can splay the leeks under cold running water to remove any soil caught among the layers. Cut the leeks into 1/2-inch circles.

Turn the oven to 425 degrees. Grease a 9-inch pie plate with one tablespoon of the butter. Melt the other 2 tablespoons of butter in a frying pan. Add the leeks and 1/3 cup water; season lightly with salt; cover and cook over low heat, stirring once or twice, until the leeks are tender, which takes 5–6 minutes. During the last couple of minutes remove the lid and increase the heat to steam off any excess liquid. Keep the leeks warm and put the greased pie plate in the oven while you make the batter.

In a mixing bowl combine the flour, sugar and 1/2 teaspoon salt. In a small bowl lightly beat the eggs with 1/4 cup of the milk. Make a well in the center of the flour mixture; pour in the eggs and stir with a fork to gradually incorporate the flour, adding the rest of the milk as you go. Finally beat for about a minute to make a smooth batter.

Spread the leeks, which should still be warm, in the hot pie dish. Immediately pour on the batter and bake for 20–25 minutes or until the edges are puffed up. Serves 6–8.

SLIT LEEKS BRUSCHETTA

Medieval cookbooks have few vegetable recipes, most likely because their ways of cooking vegetables were simple so cooks could remember how to make them without needing to write down directions. But the first cookery book in English *Forme of Cury* (*The Way to Cook*) has this recipe for slit then stewed leeks. In 1390 when the book was compiled, moist foods, including these leeks, were served on pieces of toasted bread called 'sops' or 'sippets' to soak up the juices. In this updated version the sops have become bruschetta. *Forme of Cury* was created by the cooks of Richard II's court, so we can imagine these leeks being paraded before the king and his court along with peacocks and herons and venison and other splendid dishes

> *1 large garlic clove*
> *3–4 tablespoons canola or grapeseed oil*
> *8–10 slices of French bread cut on the diagonal*
>   *about 1-inch thick*
> *1/2 tsp dried thyme*
> *4 large leeks (about 2 pounds)*
> *1/2 cup white wine*
> *salt and white pepper to taste*
> *2 tablespoons finely chopped parsley*

To make the bruschetta, slice the garlic clove into 3 or 4 slices. Put them in a small pan with 2 tablespoons of the oil over medium heat and let them cook gently without browning for 3–4 minutes. Discard them. Remove the oil from the heat and stir in the thyme. Brush the oil over the slices of bread. Toast the bread on a ridged griddle to give it stripes or under the grill. Set aside.

To make the leeks, discard all dark green parts and use only the white and the very palest green sections. Slice the leeks lengthways then slit into 1-inch matchsticks. Put them in a sieve and rinse under cold running water to remove any dirt. Pat dry with paper towels. Heat a tablespoon of oil in a saucepan over low heat. Toss in the leeks and sprinkle lightly with salt. Put the lid on the pan and cook gently, shaking the pan from time to time, for 2–3 minutes. Increase the heat to medium and add the wine. Let it bubble until it has reduced by half, then lower the heat and cook gently until the leeks are tender. Remove from the heat, taste and season with more salt if necessary and with the white pepper. Let cool to room temperature. Stir about half the parsley into the leeks. Top the bruschetta with the leek mixture and garnish with the rest of the parsley. Forget about the bruschetta and serve the leeks as a side dish if you like. Serves 6–8, fewer as a side-dish.

VICHYSOISSE

Vichysoisse sounds entirely and anciently French, but it was invented in the early twentieth century in New York by a chef called Louis Diat. He said he based it on the soups of his childhood, which he spent near the French town of Vichy – hence the name. The things that distinguish Vichysoisse from other leek and potato soups are that it's intensely creamy and thrillingly chill.

2 tablespoons butter
1 small onion, finely sliced
2 cups thinly sliced leeks, white parts only
Salt to taste
1/2 cup dry white wine
1 bay leaf

2 cups thinly sliced potatoes
1 cup heavy cream
White pepper to taste
1 tablespoon snipped chives

Melt the butter in a heavy saucepan over medium heat. Add the onions and leeks and lightly sprinkle with salt. Put the lid on the pan, lower the heat as much as possible, and let the vegetables soften for 5–6 minutes. Check once or twice, stirring as necessary to make sure they don't stick to the pan or begin to take color. Add the wine, increase the heat and let the wine bubble for a minute. Now add the potatoes, bay leaf, and 3 1/2 cups water. Simmer with the pan partly covered until the potatoes are soft. Let cool to lukewarm, then process in batches until smooth. Season to taste with more salt if necessary and a little white pepper. (On no account use black pepper as it will mar the pale appearance.) Chill in the fridge. Before serving stir in the cream. Garnish with the chives. Serves 6.

Other recipes: Leeks partner carrots in Braised Carrots and Leeks (page 31), and potatoes and fennel in Potato, Fennel and Leek Gratin (page 102).

Lettuce used to be treated very differently than it is today. A popular after-dinner treat in Shakespeare's time was lettuce suckets made by steeping the leaf ribs in successive batches of syrup – the same method used for candying orange peel. A charming book anonymously published in 1744 and called *Adam's Luxury and Eve's Cookery* has three recipes for lettuces. One is a 'ragoo' of lettuces simmered in veal gravy; the second is for lettuces stuffed with sweetbreads and meat and stewed in broth. Finally a recipe titled "To Keep Lettuce" has directions for sticking it with cloves, seasoning it with pepper, salt, and bay leaf, then covering it with vinegar. This sounds crazy until we recall that until the twentieth century, when spring and summer had passed lettuces were gone until another year. Now we have many varieties of lettuce, but fewer ways of using them apart from salads and garnishes.

FLOWERY SALAD WITH LAVENDER LIME DRESSING

Lettuces belong to the daisy family. This salad recalls their flowery heritage by combining them with colorful blossoms. Among the flowers it's possible to use are violets, pansies, pot marigolds, chiveblossoms, sage blossoms, lavender, day lilies and the nasturtiums featured in this recipe because their bright color and peppery leaves make a zingy addition. In all cases you should be certain that flowers have not been doused with garden chemicals, which is a lot easier if you use flowers from your own garden.

1 Boston or other loose leaf lettuce, washed
6–8 small or medium nasturtium leaves, washed
Petals from 4–5 pot marigolds (calendula)
Zest and juice of 1 lime
2 tablespoons light-flavored olive oil
1 teaspoon honey
Petals from 4 heads of lavender or 1/4 teaspoon culinary lavender
12 nasturtium flowers

Wash the lettuce and nasturtium leaves and tear into manageable pieces. Put them in a salad bowl and scatter on the marigold (calendula) petals. In a small bowl, whisk together the lime juice, oil, and honey. Add the lavender petals. Pour on the lettuce and toss. Scatter the nasturtiums on the salad just before serving. Serves 4–6.

M

Mushrooms conjure up fairy-tales. Their shapes are odd, their arrival mysterious. They show up on lawns overnight, peek from crevices in stone walls, nestle in blankets of fallen leaves, or gather in clusters on tree stumps and wood piles. Some have enticing flavors. Truffles and porcini, for example, are among the most expensive of foods. Others are tasteless, while some are poisonous so any wild mushrooms are to be treated with the greatest of caution. Fortunately, many varieties of mushrooms can be cultivated, and several Pioneer Valley farmers now grow shiitake and sell them in farmers' markets and through supermarkets. Foragers sometimes bring their finds to farmers' markets, so occasionally you will see baskets of morels in spring, or hen-of-the-woods, black trumpets, field mushrooms, and chanterelles in fall. In countries such as Russia, Poland, and Italy, where mushroom gathering is treated as an autumnal rite, there are traditional recipes and pairings. In Russia, mixtures of mushrooms, ideally including porcini (*boletus edulis*), are cooked in sour cream or preserved in oil. In Italy, wild mushrooms of many types are often

The Valley has many varieties of mushrooms

mixed with scrambled eggs or served with game, and in French cuisine dishes described as *à la forestiere* are garnished with mushrooms. Mushrooms also feature in Chinese and Japanese, cooking. It used to be that most of their Asian varieties did not grow here, but shiitake, a staple of Japanese cooking, is now the commonest mushroom cultivated by Valley growers.

MUSHROOM AND CHICKEN CASSEROLE

Shiitake adapt well to western dishes. Here their full flavor helps create a rich but easy casserole. Shiitake stems are too tough to eat. Cut them off but use them to flavor soups and broth. For the other mushrooms called for in this recipe you can use wild or cultivated mushrooms bought from the store or from an expert mushroom forager. However, do not use any wild mushrooms unless you are one hundred percent certain that they are edible varieties. If you prefer you can simply omit the other mushrooms and use extra shiitake.

1 tablespoon vegetable oil
8 chicken thighs or drumsticks or a mixture of the two
1 teaspoon dried thyme
1 teaspoon dried savory or oregano
1 medium-large onion, chopped
1–2 cloves garlic, finely chopped
2 medium celery stalks, washed and cut in 1/2-inch piece
4 medium carrots, peeled and cut into disks
1 cup chopped shiitake caps
6–8 ounces other mushrooms, sliced or chopped
1 1/2 cups chicken or vegetable stock
1 bay leaf
8 peppercorns
Salt to taste

Heat the oil in a large lidded pan over medium high heat. Add the chicken pieces and let them cook for 4–5 minutes or until golden on one side. Turn them over. Sprinkle with the thyme and savory or oregano and cook for another 4–5 minutes to brown the other side. Remove them from the pan. Add the onion, garlic, and celery to the pan and let them soften for 4 minutes. Now stir in the carrots, shiitake, and other mushrooms. Replace the chicken pieces in the pan, pour in the stock, add the bay leaf and peppercorns, and salt to taste. Cover the pan and simmer over low heat for 40 minutes. (Alternately cook in a 350-degree oven.) Serve with rice or potatoes. If you like you can add 2–3 large potatoes, peeled and sliced to the pan along with the chicken. Serves 4–6.

RUSSIAN-STYLE MUSHROOMS WITH SOUR CREAM AND DILL

Many Russians love hunting mushrooms, taking to the forests in autumn to collect big baskets of them, many of which they either dry or can for winter use. They call their favorite the white mushroom, known to science as *boletus edulis*. Vladimir Nabokov describes the "special boletic reek which makes a Russian's nostrils dilate – a dark, dank, satisfying blend of damp moss, rich earth, rotting leaves." If this sounds less than appetizing, we know this mushroom by its Italian name *porcini*, which means "little pigs" and possibly refers to its rich, meaty taste. Chanterelles are also popular in Russia and other European countries, and so are morels, one of the few mushrooms that pokes its head out in spring. All of them grow, though not very commonly, in our area. You can buy them occasionally, but they are expensive so for this recipe you can use shiitake. It doesn't taste the same as Russia's white mushroom but it has its own fine flavor. Mix it with other mushrooms or use it on its own. Small pots of these creamy mushrooms are sometimes served as appetizers in Russia. More often they are served over potatoes as a main dish. You could also serve this mixture in tart shells or over rice,

> *12 ounces shiitake or a mix of shiitake and other flavorful mushrooms*
> *2 teaspoons flour*
> *3 tablespoons butter*
> *2 tablespoons chopped shallots or onions*
> *Salt and white pepper to taste*

1 1/4 cups sour cream
1 tablespoon snipped dill or fennel fronds

Cut the shiitake caps into strips. (Discard the tough stems or use them to flavor soup.) Cut any other mushrooms into pieces. Toss them with the flour. Melt the butter over low heat and add the mushrooms and shallots or onions. Cook gently for 8–10 minutes with the pan partly covered. Watch to make sure the mushrooms don't catch; add a little more butter if necessary to prevent this. Season them with salt and a little pepper, then stir in the sour cream, and continue to cook slowly until the mixture just reaches simmering point. Stir in the dill or fennel, then taste, and add salt and pepper (or more dill) if liked. Serves 2 with baked potatoes, or 4 if served as a sauce.

MUSHROOM FRITTATA WITH HAM AND PEAS

Like omelets, Italian frittatas are made from beaten eggs with a filling, usually of vegetables. But conceptually frittatas and omelets are quite different. While omelets are folded and served straight from the pan, and ideally are still a bit runny in the center, frittatas are cooked more slowly and either turned in their pan or slid under a broiler to brown the surface. They could be eaten straight from the pan cut in wedges, but quite often are left to cool and served with salads, either for lunch or in smaller portions as an appetizer. Their willingness to wait around before serving makes frittatas good candidates for breakfast when there's a crowd because many other breakfast egg dishes demand to be whizzed to the table. You can also take frittatas to a picnic or a potluck because they travel cheerfully.

4 ounces shiitake mushrooms
4 ounces other mushrooms
2 tablespoons olive oil
2 tablespoons butter
3 shallots, peeled and chopped, or 1/4 cup chopped onion
1 teaspoon dried oregano
1 tablespoon chopped fresh parsley

Salt to taste
3–4 ounces ham or chicken or salami, diced
1/3 cup cooked peas
6 eggs, thoroughly beaten

Take the stems off the shiitake. (They can be saved for flavoring stock or soup). Cut the caps into 1/4-inch strips. Wash the other mushrooms to remove any soil, pat them dry with paper towel and cut in pieces. Heat 1 tablespoon of the oil with the butter in a 12-inch frying pan over low heat. Add the shallot or onion and cook for 2–3 minutes. Now add all the mushrooms, sprinkle lightly with salt, and cook gently, turning often until they have softened – about 5–6 minutes. Sprinkle them with the oregano and parsley, and stir in the ham and peas. Should the mixture be very dry add the remaining tablespoon of olive oil or more butter.

Turn on the broiler to preheat. Now pour the beaten eggs in the pan of mushrooms and continue cooking over low heat for about 5 minutes or until the eggs are set and golden brown underneath. Transfer the pan to the broiler and broil for a minute or two or until the surface is golden. The frittata can be eaten immediately divided into wedges. Serves 4 as a lunch dish; about 8 if served as an appetizer.

Other recipes: Shiitake mushrooms appear in Sirloin Tips Braised with Peas and Mushrooms on page 88 and in Japanese Pickled Radishes on page 112.

Onions may be the most widely used of our vegetables. How many recipes begin with the instruction "Chop the onions" or "Fry the chopped onions?" There must be thousands of them. And this is not just true of local cooking; most cuisines use onions as an essential flavoring element. It's hard to conceive of stews, soups, and stir fries without onions. For many a slice of raw onion is a must-have on a hamburger; for others an onion bagel is the bagel of choice, and French Onion Soup is the soup of soups. For onion lovers who want to highlight this most essential of vegetables, here are some dishes where they shine in glory.

ONION AND CARAWAY COBBLER

This cobbler was inspired by a recipe for Alsatian Onion Bread in *Judith Olney on Bread* (Crown Publishers, 1985). It is an unusual, tasty, any-time-of-day dish. Serve wedges with scrambled eggs for breakfast or brunch or with fish or meat for supper. It's especially good with beef and lamb. You could also serve it at room temperature cut in bite-size pieces with drinks. Or offer chunks of it with soup or chowder. Instead of caraway seeds, you could use 2 teaspoons of cumin seeds or fennel seeds.

2 tablespoons olive oil
3 tablespoons butter
3 cups coarsely chopped onions (2–3 large onions)
Salt and freshly ground black pepper to taste
3 teaspoons caraway seeds
1 cup all-purpose flour
2 teaspoons baking powder
1/2 cup milk
1 egg
1 cup (8-ounce container) sour cream

Put the olive oil and 1 tablespoon of butter in a medium frying pan over moderate heat. When it is fairly hot, add the onions and stir them around. Cook very gently for 18–20 minutes or until they are tender and golden. Stir in 2 teaspoons caraway seeds, and cook for another couple of minutes. Season with salt and plenty of freshly ground black pepper, then tip into a 9-inch quiche dish or pie plate, and spread into an even layer

Turn the oven to 350 degrees. In a bowl combine the flour, baking powder, 1/4 teaspoon salt. Cut the remaining 2 tablespoons butter into little bits and with your fingers rub them into the flour until it looks like coarse meal. Make a well in the center. Pour in half the milk and stir to combine with the flour mixture, gradually stirring in more milk until you have a soft dough. Knead 4–5 times and form into a ball. Then on a floured board, flatten it into a disk large enough to cover the onions. Press it to the edge of the dish, then poke it all over with a skewer or knitting needle.

Beat together the egg, sour cream, and remaining teaspoon of caraway seeds. Add 4–5 grinds of black pepper and stir it in. Pour it over the dough. Place in the oven and bake for about 30 minutes or until a skewer poked in the middle comes out clean and the surface has golden brown patches. Let stand for 5 minutes before cutting. Can also be served at room temperature. Serves 6–8.

SPANISH ONION SOUP

This is much easier and quicker than the dark and cheesy French onion soup, and just as delicious. It's particularly welcome when you have a cold — or just when the weather is cold and you feel you must steel yourself against winter.

> *6 medium-large onions (about 1 1/2 pounds, peeled and coarsely chopped)*
> *2 tablespoons extra-virgin olive oil plus more to taste*
> *1 bunch parsley*
> *1 teaspoon salt*
> *1 tablespoon cornstarch*
> *Salt and white pepper to taste*

Heat the olive oil in a large pan, add the onions and stir them around. Now add 7 cups water, 10 stems of parsley, and the salt. Cover and bring to simmering point. Let simmer for 20 minutes or until the onions are tender. If you want a smooth soup, let it cool to room temperature, discard the parsley stems, then puree or sieve in batches and return to the saucepan. If you want it chunkier, ignore this step; just simply take out the parsley.

Chop the remaining parsley. You need about threequarters of a cup. Add half of this to the soup. Mix the cornstarch to a paste with 1/4 cup cold water. Stir in some of the warm soup, then introduce this mixture back into the pan and return it to simmering point. Taste for seasoning and add salt and white – not black – pepper to taste. Serve garnished with the remaining parsley. In Spain people would drizzle in some olive oil as well. Serves 6–8.

Parsnips have two seasons: one in late fall, and the other in spring, when those that have been wintered over can be dug up. During the icy months when they are fast in the ground, they develop sugar so by March and April they taste deliciously sweet. In fall, too, parsnips taste better when they have been nipped by the frost. This is true, also, of Brussels sprouts. Another characteristic these two vegetables share is that they can divide the company into those who love them and those who definitely don't. Children usually fall in the latter category; a taste for parsnips seems to grow with age, when many people fall in love with them for the first time. One man with a parsnip mission was Dick Warner, member of Amherst's South Congregational Church, who contributed a section called Parsnip Helps to *Fiddler's Pantry*, the church's 1977 cookbook. Among his suggestions was Parsnip Pizza made by replacing the tomato sauce with a parsnip puree. He also noted, "If by chance some boiled parsnips might be left over, they can be disposed of very nicely sliced and fried for breakfast." When the church updated the cookbook in 2007, it noted, "Dick grew parsnips...distributing them on Sunday mornings at the church though sometimes they might appear on a lucky friend's doorstep."

ROAST PARSNIPS

Roast parsnips are a favorite accompaniment to roast meat in England. To make them peel medium size or largish parsnips, and slice them lengthways into 2–4 sections. Avoid giant specimens as often they are woody in the middle. Parboil them for 5 minutes in lightly salted water; drain, then tuck them in around the roasting meat, basting them with the fat. When you take the meat out of the pan to rest before carving, leave the parsnips in the pan, turn up the heat to 400 degrees, and let them brown. They do this readily because the roasting caramelizes their natural sugar.

CURRIED PARSNIP SOUP

Curry powder is an easy way to add spicy flavor to many root vegetables. Parsnips taste best when the frost has nipped them, so this is a soup for cold days

> 1 1/2 pounds parsnips, peeled and cut into chunks
> salt and pepper to taste
> 1 Granny Smith apple, peeled and cut into quarters
> 1 large onion, peeled and coarsely chopped
> 1 tablespoon butter
> 1 tablespoon oil
> 1 clove garlic, crushed
> 2–4 teaspoons medium-hot curry powder
> 1–3 teaspoons brown or white sugar
> 1/2 cup (or more to taste) half-and-half

Put the parsnips into a pan and cover with about 6 cups water. Add half a teaspoon of salt and bring to the boil. Simmer for 5 minutes then add the apple quarters and continue simmering until both parsnips and apples are tender. Drain and mash the vegetables and apple together with a little liquid or process in food processor with some liquid. In either case, gradually add the remaining liquid to make a soup. Combine the butter and oil in a small frying pan and gently soften the crushed garlic in it. Stir in the curry powder and cook for 30 seconds. The powder will absorb the oil. When this has happened, pour in about half a cup of the parsnip soup and stir well. Combine this with the rest of the soup and return it to the pan. Taste for seasoning and add salt, pepper and a little sugar as needed. Simmer for another 10 minutes, tasting from time to time and adjusting the flavor as you see fit. Finally stir in the half and half and serve. Serves 4–6.

Peas have become so common in their canned and frozen forms that it is easy to forget how delicious they are when they are fresh, and quite startling to learn that the court of King Louis XIV of France they were terribly, terribly fashionable because they were the Latest Thing from Italy – then as now the go-to place for stylish stuff. Until Italian gardeners got to work, the only previous peas were dried field peas, which were an unglamorous year-round staple for the poor. After tender Italian peas reached France, their season was eagerly awaited at court. Mme de Maintenon, mistress and also perhaps wife, of the king wrote "The impatience to eat them, the pleasures of eating them, and the joy of eating them again are the three points which our princes have been discussing these last four days." Similarly, in eighteenth-century America Thomas Jefferson and his neighbors raved about peas and competed to see whose crop would come in first. Today we have multiple varieties of peas, including peas with edible pods: sugar-snaps, which truly deserve their sweet snappy name, and snowpeas, which look like someone has ironed them because they are all pod, no pea.

PEA AND MINT SALAD

Children love this salad, and since it needs neither sharp knives nor hot stoves to prepare it, even the tiniest person can make it. It's best put together at least 30 minutes beforehand so that the mint can infuse the peas. Mint has a special affinity with peas and it's worth dropping a sprig into the water any time you are cooking them.

2 cups cooked peas
8–10 leaves fresh mint
1/2 teaspoon powdered coriander
1 cup Greek yogurt
2–3 stems of mint plus a few sprigs

Put the peas in a serving bowl. Tear up the mint leaves and stir them into the peas. Now stir the coriander into the yogurt, and then combine the two mixtures. Lay the mint stems decoratively on top and set aside in a cool place so the mint can flavor the peas. Remove large stems for serving but garnish with a few little sprigs to serve. Serves 4–6.

KEEMA CURRY WITH PEAS

Keep the curry powder light and this ground beef curry appeals to kids; for those who can handle more punch, add a little more curry powder, and for those with fireproof mouths include a dusting of cayenne.

2 cloves garlic, peeled and smashed
1 teaspoon freshly grated ginger
Pinch sugar
1 tablespoon oil
1 medium onion, peeled and chopped
1-3 teaspoons mild curry powder
1 pound lean ground beef
1 or 2 pinches cayenne (optional)
1 cinnamon stick
1 bay leaf
1 1/2–2 cups tomato sauce
1 tablespoon Worcestershire sauce
Salt to taste
2 cups shelled green peas
1–2 tablespoons chopped cilantro or parsley for garnish

Pound the garlic and ginger together along with the sugar. Add a couple of tablespoons of water. Heat the oil in a shallow pan such as a large frying pan, and stir in the garlic mixture and then the chopped onion. Fry for 2–3 minutes then move the onion to one side of the pan and put the curry powder on the exposed surface. Let it cook there for about 30 seconds, then add the ground meat, crumbling it with a wooden spoon and mixing it with the onions. When it has browned, add the cayenne (if using it) the cinnamon stick, bay leaf, and finally, 1 1/2 cups tomato sauce and the Worcestershire sauce. Stir everything together, season with salt to taste, cover the pan, and simmer over low heat for 7–8 minutes. Stir in the peas, recover the pan, and simmer for another ten minutes or until the peas are tender. Taste for flavor. You can add more salt if necessary, and also more cayenne if you really want to heat it up. Scatter the cilantro or parsley on before serving with basmati rice. The Green Bean Chutney on page 65 and the Tomato and Winter Squash Chutney on page 138 are good accompaniments. You can also offer a bowl of plain Greek yogurt. Serves 4–6.

SIRLOIN TIPS BRAISED WITH PEAS AND MUSHROOMS

Peas and mushrooms have a flavor affinity, and so do beef and mushrooms. This recipe brings them all together. Shiitake mushrooms were first cultivated in Japan in the nineteenth century. It wasn't until the 1970s that Americans learned how to raise them, and then one of the pioneers was the Delftree company of North Adams. Now the Pioneer Valley has its own shiitake growers.

> 4 pieces sirloin tip steak each about 5–6 ounces
> 1/2 teaspoon dried thyme
> 1/2 teaspoon dried oregano or marjoram
> 1 clove garlic, minced
> 3 tablespoons olive oil
> Juice of half a lemon
> 1 small-medium onion, chopped
> Salt and pepper to taste
> 1/2 cup stock or water
> 4 ounces shiitake mushrooms
> 2 cups cooked peas

Sprinkle the herbs and garlic on the sirloin tips. Drizzle with 2 tablespoons of oil and the lemon juice. Cover and let rest for 2 hours (or longer if more convenient), turning the meat over once or twice. Heat the remaining tablespoon of oil in a large frying pan and soften the chopped onion in it. Add the meat and any juices collected from it, and brown. Season the meat, then add the stock or water and the mushrooms, and cover the pan. Simmer over low heat for 10 minutes. Add the peas, cover and continue simmering for 3–4 minutes or until the peas are heated through. Adjust the seasoning. Serves 4.

Stir-fried Chicken with Snowpeas and Broccoli

STIR-FRIED CHICKEN WITH SNOWPEAS AND BROCCOLI

This Chinese-style dish is designed to make use of a cooked chicken breast left over from a roast chicken or other dish. It's perfect for two people and can be stretched for 3 or 4 simply by adding extra chicken and vegetables such as mushrooms or asparagus.

Marinade:

2 tablespoons cornstarch
2 tablespoons soy sauce
2 tablespoons rice wine or sherry or white wine
1 teaspoon sugar
1/2 teaspoon sesame oil (optional)

Other ingredients:

1/2 pound cooked chicken (about one cooked chicken breast)
6 ounces snowpeas (about 1 1/2 cups)
4 scallions
About 1/2 cup small broccoli florets

2 tablespoons canola or other vegetable oil
2 cloves garlic, minced
1 tablespoon chopped shallot or onion
1 tablespoon finely chopped or sliced fresh ginger
3/4 cup chicken broth

In a medium bowl mix the cornstarch to a paste with the soy sauce and wine. Stir in the sugar and sesame oil and half a cup of water.

Cut the chicken into strips about 2 inches long and 1/2-inch wide. Add these to the bowl of marinade and set aside for half an hour or longer if more convenient. Trim the ends from the snowpeas. Cut off and discard the roots and green leafy ends of the scallions, and slice the white and tender green parts diagonally into strips. Set them aside.

To cook, heat the canola oil in a wok or frying pan over medium heat and stir in the chopped shallot or onion, then the garlic and ginger. Stir for a minute then add the snowpeas and broccoli florets. Add about a quarter cup of water, and stir over high heat for 1–2 minutes. Now put in the scallions and the chicken and its marinade. Stir until the liquid thickens, then add half a cup of the chicken broth. Continue cooking for a couple of minutes, just until the chicken has heated through and the vegetables are cooked but still crisp-tender. Add the remaining broth if you want a thinner sauce. Serve with rice. Serves 2.

RISOTTO WITH SUGAR-SNAP PEAS AND SPRING HERBS

If you make this risotto with vegetable broth you can serve it as a vegetarian main dish. It's also a lovely accompaniment to chops or steaks or fish. (In spring asparagus or fiddleheads could be used instead of sugar-snaps.)

1 pound sugar-snap peas, washed
1/2 stick butter
1 medium shallot, finely chopped
9 ounces (about 1 cup) Arborio or Carnaroli rice
1/2 cup white wine such as Pinot Grigio

*About 2 1/2 cups hot vegetable broth or chicken
    broth if you prefer*
1/2 teaspoon salt
2 tablespoons snipped chives
1 tablespoon chopped parsley plus sprigs for garnish
1 tablespoon torn mint leaves plus sprigs for garnish
3 tablespoons grated Parmesan
*About 8 paper-thin slices Parmesan cut with a
    vegetable peeler*

    Trim off any coarse ends of the sugar-snaps. In a shallow pan heat the olive oil and butter, and when it is just beginning to foam stir in the shallot and let it cook for 2 minutes, and then add the rice and cook, stirring all the time for 3–4 minutes, making sure it is all lightly coated with the butter. Add the wine, let the mixture bubble and when most of the wine has evaporated, add a ladle full of the broth and the salt. Continue to cook over medium heat, adding more broth a ladleful at a time when the previous instalment has been mostly absorbed. After 10 minutes of cooking add the sugar-snaps, half the chives and half the torn mint. Continue cooking adding ladles of the hot broth as the liquid is absorbed, for another 8–10 minutes. Cook until the grains of rice are tender but not mushy and the sugar-snaps are also tender. Finally stir in the grated Parmesan and the rest of the chives and mint. Turn into a warmed dish, and garnish with additional parsley and mint sprigs and the Parmesan flakes. Serves 3 as a main dish; 4–5 as an accompaniment.

Other recipes: Mushroom Frittata with Ham and Peas, page 80.

Peppers must have delighted the fifteenth-century Spanish explorers who found them growing in Central and South America. As we learn in school, spices were the object of their explorations. They were vital to European cooking, but they were horribly expensive because almost all of them were imported from India or South-East Asia and their journey to Europe, whether overland or by sea, was long, expensive, and fraught by storms, pirates, and tax collectors. Finding a quicker route to the lands where spices grew would be very profitable. But while explorers and conquistadors found many riches in the Americas, spices were not high on the list. They found only three: vanilla, which is the seed pod of a Mexican orchid; allspice, which grows in the Caribbean and conveniently combines the flavor of several other spices, and peppers. Technically they are called capsicums, but the first Europeans to find them called them peppers – *pimientos* in Spanish – partly because they had fieriness akin to the familiar peppercorns, and partly because they wanted to suggest that they had found what they had come for. They were not particularly interested in sweet peppers because they lacked the heat that was in demand. But while sweet peppers lingered on the sidelines, hot peppers circled the globe, becoming essential seasonings in the cuisines of India, Thailand, parts of China and Africa, and in the form or paprika and pimiento, of Hungary and Spain.

While hot peppers are used as condiments, the sweet peppers, with their traffic-light colors, are terrific vegetables. Awash in Vitamin C, they work well in vegetable stews such as ratatouille, and make handy shapes for stuffing. It used to be that most of the peppers grown in the Valley were green bell peppers or the paler Italian frying peppers. But an August visit to a farmers' market now shows mountains of red peppers rising from foothills of yellow and orange companions. They are less astringent than green peppers, and typically cook a little faster. Those with 3 bumps on the bottom are reputedly sweeter and better for eating, while peppers with 4 bumps are firmer and better for cooking.

PEPPERONATA

Pepperonata is the most thrilling of all vegetable dishes, grabbing attention with the dazzling scarlet peppers mixed with orange and gold. Appearances don't deceive in this case: few dishes are more delicious than this Italian classic. Serve it as a part of a vegetable first course, eat it as a salad, pile it on pasta or polenta, or use it as a brilliant background to grilled meat, sausages or fish. No need to worry about the exact number of peppers and tomatoes as long as about eighty percent of the total is peppers. If you are a gardener and have a bumper harvest, you can multiply the recipe to make a large batch. You can also make it of green peppers, but they don't hold their color when cooked, so the dish looks dull and is not as luscious. Keep it in the fridge but serve at room temperature or slightly warm.

> *5 medium-large red bell peppers*
> *1 yellow or orange bell pepper*
> *4–5 tablespoons fruity olive oil*
> *1 onion, quartered and thinly sliced*
> *3 large cloves of garlic, crushed*
> *5 large local tomatoes, peeled, seeded and coarsely chopped*
> *salt to taste*
> *a sprig of basil with 5–6 leaves*
> *basil sprigs for garnish*
> *1 dozen black olives (optional)*

Halve all the peppers, remove the seeds and stems, trim the pale ribs from the inside of the peppers, and cut the flesh into 1/2-inch strips. Heat the olive oil in a large frying pan over moderate heat. Add the onion and garlic, cover the pan, and cook gently for 5–6 minutes to soften. Add the pepper strips and continue gently cooking for another 10 minutes, stirring occasionally and making sure they do not brown. Now add the tomatoes, salt to taste, and the basil sprig, cover and cook for 15–20 minutes until the peppers are tender. Check after 5 minutes and if the tomatoes are exuding a lot of juice, remove the lid and increase the heat to bubble some of it away. When the peppers are ready and most of the juice has evaporated, discard the basil sprig and transfer to a serving dish. Garnish with basil sprigs and the olives if using them. Serves 6–8.

PEPPERS STUFFED WITH RAISIN AND WALNUT PILAF

Cardamom, coriander, and thyme combine with the raisins and walnuts to give this pilaf a mild yet memorable Middle Eastern flavor. It makes a wonderful stuffing for peppers. You can also use it to stuff tomatoes or winter squash such as delicata or the rounded ends of butternut. Should you have more pilaf than vegetables, serve the leftovers as a side dish.

For the Raisin and Walnut Pilaf:

3/4 cup basmati rice
2/3 cup golden raisins
2 tablespoons butter
3 shallots or 1 small onion, finely chopped
1 teaspoon salt
2 cardamom pods, lightly crushed to break the shell
1 bay leaf
1 1/2 teaspoons dried thyme
1 teaspoon powdered coriander
2 tablespoons chopped parsley
1 large ripe tomatoes, peeled, seeded, and chopped
2/3 cup chopped walnuts

For the Peppers:

2 large red peppers, halved
2 large yellow or orange peppers, halved
1 large green pepper, halved
1 pale-green Italian frying pepper, halved
Salt to taste
2–3 tablespoons olive oil
4–5 nicely shaped bay leaves

To make the pilaf, rinse the basmati rice and put it in a bowl. Cover with water and let stand for 20–30 minutes, then drain and rinse under cold running water. In a separate bowl, cover the raisins with water and let stand.

Melt the butter in a saucepan over low heat and soften the chopped shallot or onion in it for 3 minutes. Stir in the drained rice, and add the salt, the cardamom pods, the bay leaf, and 2 cups of water. Bring to simmering point then simmer over moderate heat for 10 minutes or until the water has evaporated and the rice has swollen. Cover with a lid. Turn off the burner, but leave the pan standing on it for 5–10 minutes or until the rice is tender. Remove from the stove and discard the bay leaf and cardamom pods. Drain the raisins and stir them into the rice along with the thyme, coriander, half the parsley, and the chopped tomato. Finally, stir in all but 1 tablespoon of walnuts.

Meanwhile, while the rice is cooking heat the oven to 375 degrees and grease a shallow baking dish (such as a 9" x 13" lasagne pan) with a little of the olive oil. Sit all the pepper halves cut side up in the pan. Season them lightly with salt and drizzle a little olive oil over them. Cover the pan with foil and bake them for 35 minutes or until they have softened but still hold their shape. Remove them from the oven and reduce the temperature to 350 degrees. Fill the pepper halves with the rice pilaf. Stick the bay leaves between them or on top. Drizzle with a little more olive oil, cover the dish again and bake for a further 20 minutes. During the last 5 minutes remove the foil and scatter on the remaining tablespoon of chopped walnuts. Sprinkle with the rest of the parsley just before serving. These stuffed peppers partner any main dish, and they taste just as good – maybe even better – served at room temperature. Serves 6–8 as a side dish.

CHILI WITH MULTICOLORED PEPPERS

This chunky chili looks very jolly with its array of colorful peppers. It's flavorful but not hot-hot unless you use hot sausage and add the optional red pepper flakes. This is a great dish for Halloween or any fall get-together.

1 tablespoon of vegetable oil
3 sweet or hot Italian sausages
1 large onion, chopped
2–3 cloves garlic, minced
1 1/2 pounds lean stew beef, chopped into 1/2-inch pieces
4 tablespoons chilli powder
1 teaspoon cinnamon
1/2 teaspoon cumin powder
1 tablespoon dried oregano
Salt to taste
2 cups peeled and diced tomatoes
2 cups meat or vegetable stock or water
2 cups cooked or canned kidney or pinto beans
2 red bell peppers, deveined, seeded and cut into 2-inch strips
1 yellow bell pepper, deveined, seeded and cut into 2-inch strips
1 orange or green bell pepper, deveined, seeded and cut into 2-inch strips
1 pale green frying pepper, deveined, seeded and cut into 2 inch strips
Pinch red pepper flakes (optional)

Heat the vegetable oil in a large stew pan. Remove the sausage skins and crumble the meat into the oil. As it browns move it to one side, and add the onions and garlic. Cook over moderate heat for 4–5 minutes, then add the chopped stew beef. When it has browned sprinkle on the chilli powder, cinnamon, cumin, oregano, and salt. Add the tomatoes and stock or water, put the lid on the pan and simmer for an hour. Add the beans and all the pepper strips and simmer for another 20 minutes or until the pepper strips are tender. Taste for seasoning and add more salt if necessary. You can also add additional liquid in the form of stock, water or tomato sauce if you think it necessary, and a pinch of red pepper flakes if you want a hotter chili. Serves 8–10.

HOT RED PEPPER JELLY

The last of the local peppers are still around when the first of the local apples and Cape Cod cranberries arrive. This recipe combines them in a carnelian preserve that's good to have for the upcoming holiday season. For an hors d'oeuvre serve crackers spread with cream cheese and a bright little dollop of the jelly. Stir a spoonful into your cranberry sauce recipe to give it spiciness. Serve it at breakfast with muffins such as the Morning Glory Muffins (page 125). Give it to hostesses and friends over the holidays.

Hot Red Pepper Jelly

2 large red peppers (about 1 pound)
2–4 large jalapeño peppers
2 red-skinned apples
2 cups cranberries
About 4–5 cups sugar
Juice of 1 lemon
3–4 dried red peppers (optional)

Thoroughly wash the peppers and apples. Cut the red peppers in half and remove the seeds, ribs, and stems. Halve the jalapeños lengthwise but do not remove the seeds. Use 2 jalapeños for milder jelly; up to 4 for more heat. Take the stems from the apples but do not peel or core them. Cut each apple into about 8 chunks and put them in a large pan with the halved jalapeños and the red peppers, also cut into large chunks. Add the cranberries and 5 cups of water. Bring to a boil, then simmer for 45 minutes or until all the ingredients are soft. Let cool.

Pour everything through a sieve or a colander lined with a coffee filter. Press gently to encourage the liquid to drip through, then put a plate on top weighed down by a can of food and leave for at least 2 hours so more juice drips through.

Put a small plate in the fridge to use later for testing for a set. Now measure the liquid into a large pan. For each cup of liquid add one cup of sugar. (The mixture should fill only a third of the pan to leave room for boiling). Also add the lemon juice. Stir over low heat until the sugar has dissolved. Now boil rapidly, stirring frequently, and watching to make sure it doesn't boil over the top of the pan. To test for a set, take a spoonful and holding it over the pan pour it back in. If the last two or three drops merge together before falling off the spoon, it is probably ready. To make sure, put a spoonful on the chilled plate. Let it stand for about a minute, then tip the plate. If the blob of jelly wrinkles slightly on the surface then it's set. Pour it into sterilized jars (see page viii). If you like, you can slip a dried red pepper into each jar making sure it is at the side and therefore visible. Let stand until cooled with paper towels laid across the top to absorb steam. Put the lids on and store. You do not have to process in a water bath, which destroys color and flavor, because it has lots of sugar plus cranberries and lemon juice, which are all preservatives. Store in a cool place for up to 3 months.

Other recipes: Red Peppers are essential ingredients in the Broccoli, Red Pepper and Rosemary Quiche page 16; and red or green peppers appear in Ratatouille page 146; and Pisto, page 148. They are optional in Moroccan Seven Vegetable Tagine, page 144 and Minestrone, page 149.

Potatoes come from South America. They will grow at elevations that are too cold for corn, so they are the staple of Andean natives. When the conquistadores took them back to Europe, they gradually won acceptance as a staple crop that lived conveniently in the ground, thrived in a variety of climates, and was easy to harvest. They made it to North America in 1719, when an immigrant brought them to New Hampshire. Potatoes are now the most important vegetable crop in the world, and the workhorse of many kitchens. Recipes for potatoes abound, but often they highlight other ingredients. Vichysoisse is thought of as a leek soup, though potatoes are equally vital; the attention falls on the ground meat in shepherd's pie despite its tasty potato topping. This book has several recipes in other sections in which potatoes partner other vegetables. Here we have recipes where potatoes stand solidly in the limelight.

LEMON POTATOES

These are the perfect potatoes for serving with roast chicken, and also superb with lamb and pork. Terrific with fish too.

4 large potatoes weighing in total 1 3/4–2 pounds
Salt to taste
2 teaspoons dried oregano or herbes de Provence
1/4 cup olive oil
Juice of 2 lemons

Preheat the oven to 400 degrees. Peel the potatoes and cut each into 8 or 10 long thick chunks. Place them in a single layer in a baking dish, ideally one that can be taken to the table. Season them with salt and sprinkle with the oregano or herbs. Pour the olive oil on them and then turn so each piece is coated with the oil. Warm the lemons, halve them and then squeeze the juice over the potatoes. Finally add a cup of boiling water and transfer the pan to the oven. Bake for 1 hour or until the potatoes feel tender when poked and have absorbed the liquid. If the potatoes are not golden on top, trickle on a little more olive oil and broil for 3–4 minutes. Serves 4.

POTATO CROQUETTES WITH ROSEMARY

Potato croquettes used to be more common than they are now, but they taste as good as ever, especially served alongside roast meat or chicken. In this recipe they are flavored with rosemary. The spiky needles of dried rosemary are not what you want to find in a tender croquette, so be sure to use the softer leaves of fresh rosemary, chopped small. You need quite a lot because the texture of potatoes tends to blanket the flavors of herbs. The panko called for here is a Japanese product. It's a kind of flake used to coat Japanese dishes such as *tonkatsu*. It forms a delectably crisp and tasty coating, and is not as likely to burn as home-made breadcrumbs. Most supermarkets sell panko in their Asian food aisles. For croquettes dried breadcrumbs are traditional, but panko works better.

1 1/2 pounds potatoes, peeled (or about 3–4 cups leftover mashed potatoes)
Salt to taste
2 sprigs rosemary, each about 2 inches
2–3 teaspoon fresh (not dried) chopped rosemary leaves
2 tablespoons butter
2–3 tablespoons flour
1 egg, beaten with 1 tablespoon milk
about 3/4 cup panko
about 1/3 cup vegetable or olive oil for frying

Cut the potatoes in chunks and drop them into a pan of cold water. Add half a teaspoon of salt (or to taste), and one of the rosemary sprigs. Boil for 20 minutes or until tender. Drain and discard the rosemary sprig. Mash the potatoes with the butter and 2 teaspoons of chopped rosemary. (Or use 3 teaspoons for a stronger flavor). Let cool until you can handle without hurting yourself. Shape the potatoes into 8 to 12 sausage shapes.

Have the flour on one plate, the egg on another, and the panko on a third. First roll the potato sausages in the flour, then the egg, then the panko. Set them aside. Heat the oil in a medium-large frying pan into which the potato shapes will fit without crowding. Add them a few at a time and fry for about 6–8 minutes, turning them so they get browned all over. Serve with the remaining rosemary sprigs as a garnish. Serves 4–6.

LATKES

Latkes are pancakes of grated raw potatoes. Popular all over Central Europe they are a must-have at Hanukkah, the Jewish holiday that celebrates the recovery of the Temple after it had been occupied in the second century BCE. Most of the temple's oil was gone; there was just enough to keep the candles burning for one day. Miraculously, though, it lasted for 8 days – long enough for the Temple to be purified and rededicated. To commemorate this at Hanukkah a candle is lit every day for 8 days. As for the celebratory latkes, the potatoes are not important. They were unknown outside their South American homeland until at least 17 centuries after the rededication of the Temple. It's the oil they are cooked in that's symbolic because it recalls the miraculous oil of yore. At Hanukkah latkes are usually eaten with applesauce. They are also good as a side with meat or fish dishes, and my own favorite latkes were served in a pancake house in Cracow, Poland, where they came layered with wild mushrooms.

4 cups potatoes, peeled and grated (3–6 potatoes depending on size)
3 shallots or a small onion, finely chopped
2 tablespoons flour
1/2 teaspoon baking powder
1 teaspoon salt or to taste
1 egg, beaten
Oil for frying

Let the grated potatoes stand for 15–20 minutes to exude their liquid. Get rid of this by squeezing handfuls of the potatoes. Put them in a sieve and let cold water run over them, pressing them to get rid of as much water as possible. Mix the shallot or onions into them. (If you want a particularly oniony flavor, you can double the suggested amount). Mix the flour, baking powder, and salt and stir it into the potato-onion mixture. Finally stir in the egg.

Pour enough oil in a frying pan to cover the base liberally. Using a half-cup measure, scoop the mixture into the pan and flatten to form pancakes about 3 inches in diameter. Cook over medium heat for 5 minutes or until the bottom is a rich brown, then flip and cook the other side. Don't try to speed the cooking by increasing the heat because you might brown the outside without cooking the middle through. Serve hot from the pan. Makes 6 latkes. You can make larger latkes if you like, but typically they take a few minutes longer. And of course, you might well have to multiply the recipe. Latkes are general favorites. Serves 6.

POTATO FENNEL AND LEEK GRATIN

This dish is good for a cool evening. The flavor of the fennel goes wonderfully with fish or lamb dishes. The quantities in this recipe can be doubled or trebled to make this dish for a crowd, in which case use a lasagne pan for baking it.

1 tablespoon butter or oil
4–5 medium large potatoes, peeled and thinly sliced
Salt and white pepper to taste

2 leeks, cleaned and thinly sliced
1 large or 2 medium bulbs of fennel
1 cup half-and-half
1 cup milk
1/2 cup grated sharp cheddar, optional

Preheat the oven to 350 degrees. Grease a soufflé dish or casserole with the butter. Put in half the sliced potatoes and season them with pepper and salt. Scatter on the leeks. Trim the fennel to remove damaged outer layers, taking care to reserve the green fronds. Cut it into strips about 1 1/2 inches long and 1/2 inch wide, and chop the fronds. Put the fennel in the dish with about 2 teaspoons of chopped fronds. Season with salt and pepper. Put the rest of the potatoes on top, arranging them in a spiral pattern. Season with salt and pepper. Mix the half-and-half and the milk and pour it on top. Cover with foil or a lid, and bake for an hour. Remove the covering and test with skewer to see if the vegetables are tender. When they are done, cook for 10 minutes longer without the cover so the surface turns golden brown. If you like, sprinkle on the cheese so it melts during this 10 minutes. Let rest 5 minutes before serving scattered with some of the chopped fennel fronds. Serves 4.

TWICE-BAKED POTATOES WITH TUNA AND CORN

Here's an easy supper for two that takes advantage of local potatoes and corn. Use tuna packed in oil because it has more flavor.

2 large baking potatoes, each about 10–12 ounces
1–2 tablespoons mayonnaise
1 tablespoon chopped parsley
3/4 teaspoon fresh or dried thyme
1 can chunk tuna packed in oil
Corn kernels stripped from 1 ear of corn (about 3/4 cup)
Salt and white pepper to taste
1–2 tablespoons cream or milk
3 cherry or grape tomatoes, halved

Turn the oven to 400 degrees. Wrap the potatoes in foil and bake for 1 1/4 hours, or until they give when squeezed. Remove from the oven, discard the foil, and wearing an oven mitt so not to burn your hands, cut a thick slice longways from one side of the potatoes. Remove the flesh from the sliced-off potato pieces and put it in a bowl. Add the scooped-out flesh from the potatoes leaving shells with half-inch walls. Mash the potato with a tablespoon of mayonnaise, the parsley, and thyme. Mix in the corn, then drain the tuna – though not too thoroughly – and stir in the chunks, going gently so you don't break them up too much. Add the remaining tablespoon of mayonnaise if it seems necessary to make a softer mixture. Taste and add salt and pepper as needed. Pile this mixture back into the potato shells, mounding it high. Brush the surface of the stuffing with cream or milk (which will help it brown). Add the cherry tomato halves decoratively in the center, and bake again for 10 minutes or until golden brown on top. Serves 2.

Other recipes: Potatoes are an important partner in Indian-Style Cauliflower and Potatoes on page 39; Anglesey Eggs, page 71; Rutabaga and Potato Cake with Bacon, page 114; Tomato, Monkfish and Potato Casserole, page 134; and Cheese-Stuffed Squash Blossoms, page 122.

Pumpkins seem magical. In part that must be because we grew up with pictures of Cinderella's pumpkin coach and trusted to pumpkin jack o'lanterns to scare away evil sprites. But it's also because their very size and color seems to have been conjured by someone's wand. Certainly, rows of pumpkins curing in the fields and piles of pumpkins beckoning from farmstands and door steps are part of the magic of fall in the Valley. In the kitchen pumpkins can be enchanting too. They're familiar in soups and quickbreads, and essential in the Thanksgiving pie. But their uses are seemingly endless. Lacking the barley of their English homeland, the Pilgrims even made beer from them when they first arrived in Massachusetts.

MARINATED PUMPKIN SLICES WITH MINT

You can serve these pumpkin slices from southern Italy as an appetizer or as a side-dish. Butternut squash sliced and cut in semicircles works equally well.

1 sugar pumpkin, peeled and seeded
about 4 tablespoons olive oil
1 garlic clove, halved
1 tablespoon sugar
pinch cinnamon
several grinds black pepper
1/2 cup white wine or cider vinegar
16 small mint leaves

Cut the pumpkin into 3/4-inch slices, cutting as you would a melon. Heat the olive oil and the garlic pieces gently for 2 minutes, removing the garlic as soon as it begins to look golden. Add the pumpkin pieces, a few at a time and fry until they are tender enough to be pierced easily with a fork. Set them aside and continue cooking until all the pumpkin is done, adding more oil if it is needed. At the end of the cooking, drain any excess oil from the pan and return all the slices to it. Sprinkle with the sugar and a little cinnamon, grind on the pepper, tear half the mint leaves into bits and scatter them on top, and finally, pour on the vinegar. Leave for about 20 minutes, turning the pumpkin in the mixture after about 10 minutes. Serve slightly warm or chilled with the remaining mint leaves scattered on top. Serves 6 or more if served as one of several appetiser or antipasto dishes.

PUMPKIN BREAD WITH CRANBERRIES

This easy quickbread can be served warm for dessert with a scoop of vanilla or ginger ice cream, or do duty for muffins for breakfast or mid-morning coffee.

1 cup fresh cranberries
1 tablespoon confectioner's sugar
2 cups all-purpose flour

1 tablespoon baking powder
1 tablespoon powdered cinnamon
1 teaspoon powdered allspice
1 teaspoon powdered ginger
1 cup dark brown sugar
1 egg
2 tablespoons molasses
1/3 cup canola oil
1 1/2 cups mashed pumpkin

Preheat the oven to 350 degrees. Grease and flour a 5" x 9" loaf pan or line it with parchment paper. Halve or coarsely chop the cranberries and toss with the confectioner's sugar.

In a large mixing bowl, combine the flour, baking powder, powdered cinnamon, powdered allspice, powdered ginger, and brown sugar. Stir them thoroughly together and make a well in the center. In another bowl lightly beat the egg, then beat in the molasses, oil, and finally the mashed pumpkin. Pour this mixture into the well in the flour mixture, and stir together. Mix thoroughly then stir in the cranberries. Turn the mixture into the prepared pan. Bake in the center of the oven for 40–50 minutes, or until a skewer poked into the middle comes out clean. Cool in the pan for 20 minutes, then remove from the pan and continue cooling on a rack.

PUMPKIN CURD

This recipe has been developed from a recipe in *The Right Way to Make Jams* by Cyril Grange (Elliott Right Way Books, 1981). It has the consistency of lemon curd, though of course a totally different flavor. You could also use an orange-fleshed winter squash such as acorn, butternut, or buttercup squash instead of pumpkin. Slather the curd on breakfast muffins or the Pumpkin Bread with Cranberries in the previous recipe or use to sandwich a layer cake.

2 pounds baked and mashed pumpkin
1 large orange, zest and juice

1 large lemon, zest and juice
1/2 teaspoon cinnamon
1/2 teaspoon freshly grated nutmeg
3 cups sugar
2 sticks butter
2 large eggs, beaten

Put the pumpkin in a large bowl or the top of a double boiler. Place over a pan of simmering water making sure the bowl doesn't touch the water – or place over the bottom of the double boiler. Stir in the orange and lemon zest and juice. (Add the juice of an extra lemon for a tarter curd; or add zest and juice of 2 oranges instead of the orange and lemon for a more marked orangey flavor). Stir in the cinnamon, nutmeg and sugar. Cut the butter in pieces and stir them in too. Stir from time to time until the mixture is fairly hot – about 20 minutes. Stir a little of the hot mixture into the beaten eggs and then turn this egg-pumpkin mixture into the curd, stirring quickly and thoroughly to combine. When it thickens – about 5 minutes – take it off the heat and pour into sterilized jars (see page viii). It thickens a lot as it cools.

PUMPKIN CARAMEL CUSTARD WITH SPICED APRICOTS

After the golden turkey and a myriad vivid vegetable dishes of Thanksgiving dinner, the array of pies looks delightful – but also, perhaps, too heavy, too packed with calories. On the other hand, alternative desserts can lack a certain Thanksgivingy feel. Not this Pumpkin Caramel. Essentially it's a pumpkin pie filling bathed in caramel rather than cuddled in pastry. With its garnish of spiced apricots, it has all the aromas and colors of the season so it hits the dessert spot perfectly – but not too heavily. And not just at Thanksgiving. It's a good make-ahead finale for any festive meal.

1/2 white sugar
2 cups cooked mashed pumpkin
3/4 cup light brown sugar
1 teaspoon powdered cinnamon
1 teaspoon powdered ginger

1/2 teaspoon freshly grated nutmeg
2 eggs
12-ounce can evaporated milk

For the apricots:

6 ounces (about 1 cup) dried apricots
1/4 cup white sugar
6 allspice berries
3–4 cinnamon sticks, each about 2 inches

If you have a shallow metal, enamel, or ceramic pan that can go on the top of the stove and also into the oven, use it for this. If not use a heavy-bottomed saucepan to make the caramel.

First, to make the caramel, sprinkle the white sugar over the base of a heavy pan in an even layer. Set it on a low burner and leave it there without initially stirring. Gradually the sugar at the edge will liquefy and then the sugar in the middle will follow suit. At this point you can stir any granular sugar into the liquid sugar. Watch constantly as it changes color from yellowy to golden brown to dark brown. At the golden brown stage remove the pan from the heat. The sugar will darken one or two more shades. It will set hard so if you making it in a saucepan quickly pour it into a the pie dish you will use for baking while it is still liquid, taking care not to splash it on your hands or face.

Turn the oven to 325 degrees. Mix the mashed pumpkin with the brown sugar, cinnamon, ginger, and nutmeg. Beat the eggs with a little of the milk. Gradually whisk in the rest of the milk until the mixture is thoroughly blended, then mix this milk mixture with the pumpkin mixture. Pour it on top of the hard caramel, and place the pan in the oven. Bake for about 45–55 minutes or until a knife blade slid into the center comes out clean. Remove and cool overnight or for at least 8 hours. Before serving let it come to room temperature.

Meanwhile prepare the apricots by putting them in medium saucepan with enough water to cover by 1 inch. Add the sugar, allspice berries, and one cinnamon stick. Simmer until the apricots have softened. Let cool in their liquid, then remove them and the allspice berries with a slotted spoon.

For serving run a palette knife between the pumpkin and the side of the pan. Place a serving plate upside down on top of the pan, then holding on to both pan and plate, invert the pan and give it one or two sharp shakes. If the pumpkin custard doesn't fall onto the plate, tip it right way up and loosen it a bit more with a palette knife. Pile some of the apricots in the center of the custard and garnish with the allspice berries and three remaining cinnamon sticks. Cut the custard into wedges and serve with two or three apricots on the side. Serves 8–10.

Other Recipes: You can use pumpkin instead of butternut in the Butternut Caribé recipe on page 21 and Butternut Sautéed with Apples and Onions on page 23. Pumpkin can also be used in the Tomato and Winter Squash Chutney on page 138.

Purple-top Turnips have endeared themselves to gardeners by coming early in the year – usually by June – when most other things are still finding their feet. Like radishes, when eaten raw they have the mustardy bite typical of the cabbage family. For this reason fresh-from-the-garden purple-tops are good sliced and served with other raw vegetables and dips. The heat disappears when they are cooked. Often turnips are a chorus-line vegetable in soups and stews, but they are good in solo parts on their own too. In France the first purple-top turnips are the traditional thing to serve with spring lamb.

CRUMBED PURPLE-TOPS

This easy and tasty recipe can be varied by using different herbs and choosing crumbs from different kinds of bread. They are good with roast meat, and even better if you use some of the fat from the meat instead of the butter. The idea is to give the turnips a crunchy accent; you are not trying to bread them so don't bother trying to get the crumbs to cling.

1 pound (about 4) medium purple-top turnips, peeled
1 tablespoon oil

1 tablespoon butter
Salt and pepper to taste
About 1/2 cup coarse fresh breadcrumbs
1 teaspoon fresh rosemary or dried thyme
2 teaspoons snipped chives

Cut each turnip into 6 or 8 thickish wedges depending on the size. Drop them in a pan of boiling salted water. Cook for 8 minutes or just until they are tender. Do not overcook. Drain. Put the oil and butter in a frying pan over medium heat, add the drained turnips and stir them around. Season with salt and pepper, then add the crumbs, the rosemary or thyme, and half the chives. Cook stirring until the crumbs have absorbed the fat and become golden. Serve garnished with the last of the chives. Serves 4–6.

MAPLE-GLAZED TURNIPS

This sweet vegetable dish is best served with pork or lamb. It's good, too, with grilled foods.

1 pound (about 4) medium purple-top turnips, peeled
1 tablespoon canola or olive oil
1 tablespoon butter
2 tablespoons maple syrup
1 teaspoon thyme or summer savory

Cut each turnip into 6 or 8 thickish wedges depending on the size. Drop them in a pan of boiling salted water and cook for 8 minutes or just until they are tender. Do not overcook. Drain them. In a skillet over medium heat combine the oil and butter. When there's a light sizzle from the pan, stir in the maple syrup and then the purple-top turnip pieces. Cook over medium-high heat for about 5 minutes, turning the pieces over occasionally until they are golden brown all over. Sprinkle in the thyme or savory during the last few seconds. Serves 4–6.

Radishes taste at their very best straight from the earth. What gardener has not pulled one up, rubbed away the soil, and just popped it in? Their rosy shades of red look enticing too. No wonder sellers bunch radishes into posies. At the other end of the radish family scale there are daikon, long white radish looking more like parsnips than their little red cousins. Though they don't look so pretty, they are equally peppery. You can occasionally find black radish too. They're popular in eastern European cookery, and they are very hot. All radishes get their heat comes from mustard oil. You can also taste it in cabbage stalks because mustard, radish, and a great many more vegetables belong to the cabbage family.

In Japan finely grated daikon is used as a marinade for tenderizing foods and to remove strong smells from fish. In France, radishes are often served with the nicest of their little leaves still intact and a dish of butter so people can add a little dab. It softens the fieriness but more importantly it tastes delicious. In the southern states radishes are grated and served on tiny tea sandwiches. These are also delicious but you must eat them right away before the juice can leak out of the radish shreds and sog the bread.

Japanese Pickled Radishes

JAPANESE PICKLED RADISHES

This pickle is for eating right away rather than for storage — though leftovers are fine in the fridge for a couple of days. It's a natural with Japanese foods such as sushi and tempura.

2 daikon radish (about 10 inches long)
8 large red radishes
1–2 large shiitake mushrooms
1-inch chunk ginger, grated
1 small dried red chili (optional)
2 teaspoons salt
1 tablespoon sugar
3 tablespoons rice vinegar
1–2 teaspoons soy sauce

Wash all the radishes. Slice the red radishes thinly into rounds. Grate the daikon. Wash the shiitake and slice into very thin strips. Put them with the radishes in a bowl and add the grated ginger. Sprinkle with the salt. Rub the salt into the vegetables with your fingers for a minute or two, then add the red chili cut it into 3 – 4 pieces if you are using it. Cover the vegetables with a plate or suitably sized board and weight it down. (A full can of food works well as a weight.) Leave for about an hour then drain off the liquid that will have accumulated. Tip the radishes and mushrooms into a sieve and rinse under cold running water. Put them in serving bowl. Stir the sugar into the vinegar until it has dissolved. Add the soy sauce, using one or two teaspoons as you prefer. Pour this over the radishes. Serve as a relish.

RADISH AND SPINACH SALAD WITH MAPLE-MUSTARD DRESSING

The first local greens taste wonderful, baby spinach especially so. This salad lends itself to many variations. You could add arugula, tender radish leaves, or some sliced mushrooms or bacon cut in half-inch bits. Black olives are another possibility. Dry mustard powder such as Colman's or a Chinese brand is what you need to give the dressing its edge; Dijon doesn't do it.

For the salad:

about 8–10 loosely packed cups baby spinach leaves
20 medium-sized radishes
2 tablespoons snipped chives

For the dressing:

2 tablespoons maple syrup
1/2 teaspoon dry mustard powder
2 teaspoons white vinegar or more to taste
2 tablespoons olive oil
salt to taste

Wash the spinach well, and pick it over, discarding tough stalks and leaves. Dry it on paper towels. Wash and dry the radishes then slice them thinly. To make the dressing, put the maple syrup into a small bowl and stir in the mustard powder until you have a smooth mixture. Add the lemon zest, lemon juice, oil, and a little salt. Whisk lightly then taste. Add more salt if necessary. Put the radish slices in the salad bowl with 1 tablespoon of the chives and 1 tablespoon of the dressing. Mix. Add the spinach and the remaining dressing and toss. Sprinkle the remaining chives on top. Serves 4.

Rutabaga rarely takes center stage in food articles and it almost never appears on restaurant tables. The problem seems to be that if left hanging about in water it gets soggy and develops a sulphuric taste – a common habit with its fellow members of the cabbage family. Avoid this by cooking it only until tender – 20 minutes in boiling salted water. In his charming poem "Rutabagas: A Love Poem" James Silas Rogers says rutabaga leave "the tongue with a rumor of something underground and dark." Just so – and not everyone likes it. But rutabaga is more versatile than it might seem. Serve it mashed on its own or mixed with an equal amount of mashed potato with plenty of pepper or a little nutmeg, or try it in one of the following recipes.

VANILLA-SCENTED RUTABAGA

I have seen recipes for vanilla-scented rutabaga in books written by Danish, Finnish, and Norwegian writers, so this is definitely a Scandinavian way of cooking a Scandinavian vegetable.

> 1 1/2–2 pounds rutabaga peeled and diced
> Salt to taste
> 2 tablespoons butter, melted plus a knob of butter
>   for serving
> 1 teaspoon vanilla extract
> 1/4 teaspoon powdered allspice, or to taste
> Freshly ground black pepper to taste

Bring a saucepan of lightly salted water to the boil. Add the rutabaga and cook for 20–30 minutes or until soft. Drain well. Puree it in a food processor or mash by hand, blending in the melted butter, the vanilla extract, and the allspice. Taste and add more salt or allspice plus freshly ground pepper if you would like it. Serve with an extra knob of butter. Serves 6.

RUTABAGA AND POTATO CAKE WITH BACON

The rosy strips of bacon set off the primrose-colored mixture of rutabaga and potatoes charmingly.

> 4 medium potatoes (about 1–1 1/4 pounds)
> half a large rutabaga (about 1–1 1/4 pounds)
> 1 teaspoon salt or more to taste
> 3–4 tablespoons hot milk
> pepper to taste
> 1 tablespoon butter
> 6 slices bacon
> 2 tablespoons chopped fresh parsley or chives

Peel the potatoes, cut into chunks, put them in a pan, cover with cold water, add half a teaspoon of salt, and boil for 20–25 minutes until tender. Drain. Add the hot milk and mash until smooth.

While the potatoes are cooking, peel the rutabaga, cut it into chunks, put them in a pan of cold water with half a teaspoon salt, bring to the boil and cook for 20 minutes until tender. Drain. Mash or process in a food processor until smooth, adding a generous seasoning of pepper and the butter. Combine the potatoes and rutabaga. Taste and add more salt and pepper as necessary then mix in a tablespoon of the parsley.

Also while the vegetables are cooking, trim off excess fat from the ends of the bacon slices. Cook the bacon in a frying pan until it is gold. Do not let it become brown or crisp.

Lightly grease a 9-inch pie dish with a little of the fat that has run from the bacon. Arrange the bacon slices criss-cross in the pan so they divide it into 6 sections. Pile the potato-rutabaga mash on top and smooth the surface down. Bake for 20–30 minutes or until the surface is dry. For serving, run a knife around the edge of the pan to loosen the mixture. Wearing oven mitts to protect your hands, put a warmed platter on top of the pan, and invert it onto the platter. Shake sharply to release the rutabaga-potato cake if necessary. Sprinkle with the rest of the parsley and serve. Serves 6.

Other recipes: Rutabaga pairs with carrots in Chopped Carrots and Swede page 32.

Spaghetti Squash is weird. Instead of having the smooth-textured flesh of butternut, acorn, and its other cousins in the winter squash family, it comes out of its skin in spaghetti-like strands. To get the spaghetti effect, you can either halve it and bake it at 350 degrees for about 45 minutes or boil it for about 30–40 minutes. In either case you know it's done when you can pierce it easily with a skewer. Slice the squash from the stem end down to the base (not across the middle), discard the seeds in the center, and lightly scrape the strands of flesh from the skin. You can serve it with any sauce you would use for real spaghetti, or simply toss it with parsley or other herbs.

SPAGHETTI SQUASH AND SMOKED MACKEREL SALAD

Smoked mackerel blasts this salad with lively flavor. It's rich too, so you do not need an oil-based dressing. You will need the strands from half a medium spaghetti squash so you could cook one and eat half of it hot with a sauce or as a side dish, saving the other half to eat cold in this salad. Of course, to serve a lot of people, use a whole squash and double the other ingredients in this recipe.

Strands from half a medium spaghetti squash
    (about 2 cups of cooked squash)
7 or 8-ounce package peppered or herbed smoked
    mackerel
1 cup cold cooked green beans cut in 1-inch pieces
2 tablespoons chopped fresh parsley
1 tablespoon snipped fresh chives
16 cherry or grape tomatoes, halved
Salt if needed
1–2 lemons

Cook the spaghetti squash in boiling water for about 30 minutes or until it is tender when pierced by a skewer. Let it cool to a handleable temperature, then cut it in half longways. Remove and discard the seeds. With a fork scrape the flesh so it emerges in spaghetti-like strings. You need 2–3 cups of the strands. Let them get cold,

Packages of smoked mackerel generally contain 2 fillets. Break one up into 1-inch bits. Toss these with the beans, parsley, and chives, then toss with the spaghetti squash and tomato halves. With a zester, scrape the zest from one lemon and add to the mixture. Squeeze on the lemon juice and toss again. Taste. The mackerel is salty so you may not need more, but add it if necessary. Pile the mixture on plates and break the remaining mackerel fillet into large chunks and put a piece on top of each serving. Add a lemon wedge. Serves 2 as a main dish salad; 4 as an appetizer.

Spinach keeps us strong to the finish sings Popeye the Sailorman. Its nutritional advantage is a mass of Vitamin A, but its real virtues are culinary rather than nutritional. It has flavor without stridency, so it's an amiable partner to other foods including eggs, cheese, and various sorts of pastry. Its oddity – one shared with some other leafy greens – is that a massive panful collapses down to an astonishingly small volume because it exudes so much juice. It therefore needs no more water to cook in than that clinging to the leaves after it's washed. Also, for many recipes, it should be squeezed really hard so that it doesn't end up as a soggy mess on the plate. Medieval cooks made good use of the emerald juice of spinach. They loved colored food and spinach juice was their go-to source for green dye.

Because it grows low to the ground spinach can get dirty, especially in rainy weather. It needs pernickety washing in several changes of water. When you think it's clean, let it stand in a sink of cold water for about 20 minutes. With a bit of luck, any remaining grit will drift off the leaves and down to the bottom.

Spinach and Salmon Roulade

SPINACH AND SALMON ROULADE

The pinwheel effect of a roulade might look as if it can be achieved only with an advanced culinary degree, and reading the instructions for doing it may well not persuade you otherwise. In fact, it's easy and not particularly time consuming. The fillings for this spinach roulade can be varied: tuna, chopped ham or mushrooms can replace salmon, or you can use ratatouille or pisto. Recipes for the latter are on pages 146 and 148 respectively.

For the roulade:

8 ounces spinach (about 5–6 cups raw or 3/4–1 cup cooked)
Salt to taste
3 tablespoons butter
3 tablespoons all-purpose flour
1/2 cup milk
4 eggs separated
1/2 cup Parmesan
A few gratings of nutmeg

For the salmon filling:

1 cup cooked salmon or canned red salmon
1 tablespoon mayonnaise
3/4 cup whipped cream cheese
Zest of 1 lemon
1 tablespoon grated Parmesan

Wash the spinach, discarding any tough stems. Put the wet leaves in a large pan, sprinkle lightly with salt but add no more water. Put over low heat and cook for 2–3 minutes, stirring once, until the leaves are tender. Drain very thoroughly, then squeeze the cooled spinach in your hands as tightly as possible to remove as much liquid as you can. Chop and set aside.

Preheat the oven to 400 degrees. Line a 9" x 12" jelly roll pan with parchment paper and grease the edges with oil.

To make the roulade, melt the butter in a pan over low heat. Off the heat stir in the flour one tablespoon at a time. Return to the low heat and stir in half the milk. Continue stirring and add the rest of the milk as the mixture thickens. Off the heat beat in the egg yolks one at a time, and finally mix in the Parmesan and spinach. Grate in a little nutmeg. Beat the egg whites until they form soft clouds rather than dry peaks. Fold them into the Parmesan mixture. Spread the mixture in the prepared pan. Bake in the center of the oven for 15 minutes or until the surface is dry, very slightly browned, and springs back when you press it lightly with your finger. Remove the pan from the oven and run a knife round the edge to make sure the roulade has not stuck. Spread a clean smooth-textured kitchen towel on the counter and invert the pan on it so the roulade falls out. Strip off and discard the parchment paper. Now flip the edge of the towel onto the long side of the roulade and roll the towel up so that the roulade ends up rolled inside it. Leave it for 5–10 minutes. During this time the towel will absorb the steam from the hot roulade, and it will get used to be rolled up.

Make the filling while the roulade is in the towel Roughly mash the salmon and mix it with the mayonnaise, cream cheese, and lemon zest. Unroll the roulade, which will now be a bit curved and gently spread the filling in it leaving a 1-inch space at the long edge farthest from you. Reroll the roulade going gently but firmly. Trim off a very thin slice from each end to give a tidy finish. Put it on a long serving plate or board seam side down. Sprinkle with the Parmesan and garnish with watercress or basil and perhaps some cucumber slices or cherry tomatoes. Serve at room temperature, cutting slices with a serrated bread knife. Leftovers keep extremely well, Simply wrap it in plastic wrap and store in the fridge. Serves 4–6.

SPANISH SPINACH

I call this is Spanish spinach because it has the flavors of Spain: oranges, almonds, and olive oil from the vast groves of Andalucia.

2 pounds spinach, washed
2 tablespoons Spanish olive oil
Salt to taste
2 Valencia oranges, one cut into wedges
3 tablespoons sliced almonds, toasted (see page ix)

Discard any battered leaves and coarse stems from the spinach. Put it in a pan with only the water clinging to it from having been washed. Cover the pan and cook over low heat, stirring once or twice until the spinach has wilted. Drain it.

Heat the olive oil over medium heat and stir in the spinach, adding a little salt to taste. Stir in the zest of one of the oranges. Cook for a minute or two, stirring most of the time, until excess water has evaporated from the spinach, then squeeze juice to taste from the zested orange. Transfer to a serving bowl. Scatter on the almonds, and arrange the orange wedges attractively on or around the spinach. Serves 4-6.

FISH FLORENTINE

The word Florentine in a French recipe signals that the dish has a base of spinach and a cheese sauce. Sole Florentine is a classic and sole could be used in this recipe, but any good white fish such as cod, haddock or halibut is equally nice – halibut especially so.

1 pound spinach
Salt to taste
Freshly grated nutmeg to taste
4 fillets (each 5–6 ounces) white fish such as sole, haddock or cod
Cheese sauce made with Gruyère (see page xi)
1–2 tablespoons grated Parmesan

Wash the spinach in plenty of cold water. Discarding any battered leaves and coarse stems, put it in a saucepan with just the water clinging to the leaves and a seasoning of salt. Cover and cook over medium heat for 4–5 minutes or until the spinach has wilted and is tender. Drain off any liquid, pressing the spinach firmly to make it as dry as possible.

Preheat the oven to 350 degrees and grease a shallow baking dish of roughly 1 1/2 quarts capacity. Put in the spinach and dust it lightly with freshly grated nutmeg. Place the fish fillets on top and season lightly with salt and white pepper. Pour the cheese sauce over the fish and spinach and sprinkle with the grated Parmesan. Bake for 18–20 minutes. Serve with potatoes or carrots. Serves 4.

Other recipes: You need spinach for the Radish and Spinach salad with Maple Mustard Dressing on page 112, and you can use spinach instead of Swiss chard in the meatball recipe on page 130, and in Swiss Chard and Lentil Soup on page 129, and Minestrone on page 149.

Squash blossoms are treated as a vegetable in Mediterranean countries. Zucchini are generally sold with their blossoms still intact, and sometimes the flowers are sold on their own. People take them home and quick, before they wilt, stuff them, either with a cheese mixture as in the following recipe, or with a rice pilaf such as the Raisin and Walnut Pilaf used for stuffing peppers on page 94. Mexicans also appreciate squash blossoms, which they make into soup. This is a good recipe for gardeners who have a steady supply of squash blossoms throughout the summer. You can use blossoms from other kinds of squash, including winter squashes and pumpkins, in the same way.

CHEESE-STUFFED SQUASH BLOSSOMS

This flower has male and female forms. The female produces the vegetable, so don't use these flowers. You can pick all but a few of the male blossoms without fear that you're losing a crop sometime down the road. Identify male blossoms by their earlier arrival and their narrow stems. The female flowers have an enlarged base, which eventually becomes a squash. The quantities in this recipe are approximate; the amounts needed depend on the number of blossoms you have.

1 cup mashed potato
2–3 tablespoons Parmesan
1 cup grated sharp Cheddar or crumbled feta
2 teaspoons snipped chives or mint
salt, pepper, and cayenne to taste
2–3 tablespoons milk
12 or more blossoms from zucchini or squash plants
2–3 tablespoons flour
1 egg
1 cup dried bread crumbs
Oil for frying

In a bowl mix the potato with the Parmesan and the Cheddar or feta. Add the chives if using Cheddar, the mint if using feta. Season to taste with salt and pepper and a tiny pinch of cayenne.

Stir well to mix thoroughly, adding a tablespoon of milk if necessary to make a mixture that you can stir – though not one that's sloppy. Check the blossoms for any six-legged inhabitants and rinse gently. Put a spoonful of filling inside, pressing it gently into the throat of the flower. Gently but firmly twist the ends of the petals to enclose the filling. When all the flowers are filled, put the flour on one plate, the egg beaten with a tablespoon or so of milk on another, and the bread crumbs on a third. Roll each flower gently, first in the flour, then in the egg mixture and then in the bread crumbs. Let them rest for 20 minutes (or longer if more convenient) so they can firm up. To cook, heat a quarter inch of olive oil in a large frying pan over medium heat. Place the blossoms in the pan (in batches if necessary to leave some space between them). Cook for about 4 minutes rolling them so they become golden brown all over. Place them on a warmed platter and cover or put in a warmed oven to stay warm until all are done. Serve with drinks or as part of an antipasto platter or as a garnish to steak or other dishes. Serves 6–10 depending on the number of blossoms available.

Summer Squash is not unique in ripening in the summer. So why does the yellow form of summer squash earn the epithet of the season? I think it must be that its sunshiney color gives it better claim that the dark green of its zucchini cousin. It's also sometimes called crookneck because the thin end sometimes hooks round a bit. It can be used in any recipe that calls for zucchini, and sometimes it's the best choice because while both vegetables cook down into an unappetizing mush if they are cooked too long – which is not very long at all – summer squash is a bit sturdier than zucchini. Its pretty color is worth high-lighting, so be sure to include it among grilled vegetables or crudités.

THE SHAKERS' HEAVENLY SQUASH

This dish is all about yellow. Yellow summer squash with yellow corn baked in a yellow sauce of eggs and cheese. It's a festival of summer color and light. The recipe comes from the Shakers, a nineteenth-century religious community whose villages dotted New England. You can visit one of them at Hancock just outside Pittsfield, where the Shakers specialized in growing herbs and producing packaged seeds.

About 6 small summer squash (1 1/2 pounds total weight)
2 teaspoons salt
2 ears corn, shucked
1 small clove garlic, minced
1 teaspoon fresh thyme
3 eggs
3/4 cup milk
2 cups grated Vermont sharp Cheddar
pepper and salt to taste

Preheat the oven to 375 degrees, and grease a 1 1/2 quart baking dish. Wash the squash and chop into 1/2-inch pieces. Put them in a colander, sprinkling with salt as you go. Let stand for 45 minutes, then rinse off the liquid that will have gathered on the surface and dry. Cut the corn from the cobs and mix the kernels with the squash, garlic, and thyme in the prepared baking dish. Whisk together the eggs and milk, season with pepper and just a little salt, then stir in all but a couple of tablespoons of the cheese. Pour over the squash and corn. Sprinkle the reserved cheese on top. Cover with foil and bake for 40 minutes or until the squash feels tender when prodded with a fork. For a browned top remove the foil during the last 8–10 minutes of baking. Serves 2–3 as a vegetarian main dish; 4–6 as a side dish.

Other recipes: You need summer squash in Green Bean Chutney on page 65; in Ratatouille, page 146; Minestrone, page 149; and in Sweet Potatoes and Italian Sausage Sautéed with Summer Vegetables, page 128.

Sweet Potatoes are an American native, unknown in Europe until Columbus took them to Spain. They were the first potatoes to arrive in Europe, so when Shakespeare's Falstaff ran up a bill for potatoes and sack it was sweet potatoes he was pigging out on, not the white ones, which botanically speaking belong to an entirely different family. Sack was the Elizabethan name for sherry, and Falstaff was right to note its affinity for sweet potatoes. A tablespoon added when mashing them gives a mysterious background flavor.

Sweet potatoes are particularly associated with southern soul cooking because they like growing in the sub-tropics and tropics. Frost is their enemy in New England, but in recent years locally grown sweet potatoes have been showing up in farmers' markets as producers find ways to shield them from the cold. Between 3 and 6 percent of a sweet potato is sugar, and they develop more when they are heated, either by being stored in a warm spot, which suits them much better than a fridge, or in the early stages of cooking, when enzymes are converted to sugar. This makes them good in desserts and baked goods. No wonder Falstaff said "Let the sky rain potatoes."

MORNING GLORY MUFFINS

People are finicky over breakfast. Some hate it; others must have the same thing every day; some say they like it but don't have time for it. Nutritionists agree that we need something that powers us up for the day. These Morning Glory muffins fulfil that need. Sweet potatoes and bananas provide a wealth of vitamins and minerals, while whole-wheat flour, oats, and eggs have protein to fuel the morning. You can use leftover mashed sweet potatoes, or bake one very large sweet potato and mash it especially for the recipe. Sweet potatoes belong to the same *Ipomoea* genus that includes the lovely blue morning glories that twindle up fences and mailboxes in late summer. These muffins taste pretty glorious too.

Morning Glory Muffins for a satisfying breakfast

1 cup mashed sweet potato (could be leftovers)
1 very ripe banana, peeled and mashed with 1 teaspoon sugar
2 eggs, lightly beaten
1/2 cup canola oil
1 1/2 cups all-purpose flour
1/2 cup whole wheat flour
1/2 cup rolled oats
4 teaspoons baking powder
3/4 cup dark brown sugar
1/4 teaspoon mace or freshly grated nutmeg
1/2 teaspoon cinnamon
2–4 tablespoons milk or as needed
1/2 cup chopped walnuts

Preheat the oven to 400 degrees. Grease a 12-hole muffin pan or line the holes with cupcake liners.

In a medium bowl, stir together the sweet potato, banana, eggs, and oil. In a large bowl, mix the two flours, oats, baking powder, brown sugar, mace or nutmeg, and cinnamon. Make a well in the center of these dry ingredients and pour in the sweet potato mixture. Stir quickly to combine but do not over beat. If the mixture is very stiff – too stiff to stir easily – add milk a little at a time until you get a soft – but not sloppy – dropping consistency. Stir in walnuts. Spoon into the prepared muffin pan, filling each cup full. Bake for 18–20 minutes or until a toothpick or skewer poked into the middle comes out clean. Makes 12.

SWEET POTATO MERINGUE PIE

Sweet potato pie is a southern classic. This meringue-topped version could appear at Thanksgiving or any festive meal.

Pie Shell:

1 1/2 cups all-purpose flour
4 tablespoons chilled butter
2 tablespoons chilled lard or shortening

Filling:

4 small-medium sweet potatoes (about 1 pound),
  cooked and mashed
4 tablespoons butter, melted
3 eggs, separated
3/4 cup brown sugar
Zest 1 orange
1 teaspoon powdered coriander
1/2 teaspoon cinnamon
1/2 cup whipping cream
4 tablespoons white sugar

To make the pie shell, rub the butter and lard or shortening into the flour. Or process briefly together in a food processor. When the mixture looks like fine bread crumbs make a well in the center, and add 2 tablespoons chilled water. Stir into the mixture and pull to combine into a dough. If necessary to achieve this, add more chilled water a teaspoon at a time. Knead once or twice then form into a disc, wrap in plastic wrap and hold in the fridge for 2 hours. Before rolling it out grease a 9-inch pie dish. Roll out the pastry on a cold surface and fit it carefully into the dish. Do not trim off the edges at this point. Hold it in the fridge while you make the filling.

Preheat the oven to 400 degrees. You should have 1 1/2 cups or a little more of mashed sweet potato. In a bowl mix it with the melted butter, the egg yolks, brown sugar, coriander, cinnamon, and cream. When it is smooth pour it into the prepared pie shell. Now trim off any excess crust and bake for 18–20 minutes or until the crust has become golden.

Meanwhile, in a large bowl beat the egg whites until foamy and stiff. Beat in one tablespoon of white sugar until it has dissolved and the egg whites look glossy. Then beat in the rest of the sugar in the same way, adding one tablespoonful at a time and beating until glossy after each addition.

Remove the pie from the oven and lower the heat to 350 degrees. Pile the egg white on the sweet potato filling, spreading it so that it meets up with the edge of the crust leaving no exposed filling. Bake for 5 minutes, then reduce the heat to 300 degrees and bake for 15–20 minutes more. This pie is best served lukewarm or at room temperature. Serves 8.

SWEET POTATOES AND ITALIAN SAUSAGES SAUTÉED WITH SUMMER VEGETABLES

2 tablespoons olive oil
3 sweet Italian sausage and 1 hot Italian sausage, total weight 1 pound, cut in bite-sized pieces
1 small onion, chopped
1 pound sweet potatoes, peeled and cut in 1-inch cubes
1 small red pepper, cut in strips
1 medium yellow summer squash, cut in 1-inch cubes
1 large ripe tomato, peeled, seeded and chopped
About 10 rosemary leaves roughly chopped
1/2 cup cooked peas or cooked green beans cut in 1/2-inch pieces
1 cup chicken or vegetable stock
1 tablespoon chopped parsley or snipped chives

Heat the oil in a sauté pan or frying pan over medium heat. Add the onions and sausage pieces, and cook for about 5 minutes until the sausage pieces have browned on the outside. Remove them to a plate and set aside. Add the sweet potato cubes and pepper strips to the pan. Season lightly with salt, toss lightly then cover the pan and cook over moderate heat for 5 minutes or until the sweet potatoes are beginning to soften. Return the sausage to the pan along with the yellow squash and sauté for 5 minutes, taking care the onions don't brown. Add the chopped tomato, rosemary, peas or beans, the stock and half the parsley, and sauté until the tomatoes are tender and the peas or beans heated through. Serve with rice, cous cous, or pasta. Serves 4.

Swiss Chard is a cut-and-come-again vegetable that provides a crop from early summer through to late fall. In fact, it produces two crops: crinkly but tender green leaves that taste a bit like spinach, and crisp stems, which may be white, lemon, pink, or deepest ruby, that taste like mild beets. Indeed, Swiss chard belongs to the beet family though its business end is above ground rather than below. The name is a mystery because it has no special association with Switzerland. But it's a favorite in France, Italy, and especially in Croatia, where restaurants throw in a dish of it with almost every meal. The people of the eastern Mediterranean like it too, and in Australia the stalks are prized under the name silver beet. The world thus abounds in recipes for this handy vegetable, plus you can cook the leaves in any way you would cook spinach or kale.

SWISS CHARD AND LENTIL SOUP

This soup is Turkish in inspiration. Like most soups, it does not require exact amounts of each ingredient, so feel free to add more chard if your garden is producing it like mad.

3/4 cup lentils
2 tablespoons olive oil
1 large onion, chopped

3–4 cloves garlic, finely chopped
1 stalk celery, cut in 1/2-inch slices
2 carrots, peeled and sliced
1–2 cups chopped peeled tomatoes
2 quarts vegetable or meat broth or water
1 bay leaf
2 teaspoons dried oregano
1 teaspoon powdered allspice
Salt to taste
Pinch hot pepper flakes (optional)
1 bunch (about 12 stems with leaves) Swiss Chard

Put the lentils in a small bowl and cover with water. In a large soup pan, heat the oil and stir in the onions, garlic, and celery. Cook gently for about 5 minutes or until they have softened. Stir in the carrots and tomatoes, then the broth, bay leaf, oregano, allspice, and half a teaspoon of salt. Drain the lentils and add them to the pan along with a pinch of hot pepper flakes if you are using them. Cover and simmer for half an hour or until the lentils are quite tender. Meanwhile, wash the chard and cut the stems into 1-inch pieces. Cut the leaves into bite-size bits. Add the stem pieces to the soup and simmer for 10 minutes, or until they are tender, then add the leaf pieces and simmer for another 5 minutes. Taste for seasoning and add more salt and allspice if necessary. Serves 8.

SWISS CHARD AND PORK MEATBALLS

Swiss chard lightens and flavors these meatballs. Other tender greens such as spinach or beet greens could also be used. This dish freezes well, so you can double the amount and freeze some for winter.

3 tablespoons oil
1 cup chopped onion
1 large clove garlic, minced
1 pound ground veal or pork
1/2 pound ground beef

2 teaspoon dried sage
2 teaspoon dried oregano
1/2 teaspoon allspice
Salt and pepper to taste
2 cups cooked Swiss chard leaves, chopped
About 3 tablespoons flour
2 cups fresh or canned peeled, seeded, and diced tomatoes
2 medium bay leaves
1 teaspoon dried oregano
2–3 tablespoons chopped parsley or chives for garnish

Heat half the oil in a frying pan over moderate heat and cook the chopped onion and garlic in it, stirring often, for 4–5 minutes or until limp and softened. In a large bowl combine the onion mixture with the veal or pork and the beef. Mix briefly then add the sage, oregano, allspice, and salt and pepper to taste. Mix thoroughly, then mix in the chard. At this point do not stir in the chard so well that is disappears: it should be a noticeably green presence. Take a small portion of the mixture and form it into a patty about the size of a dollar coin, Fry it on both sides and then taste it. Add more of any of the herbs or seasonings to the mixture if you think it needs it. Then form into balls the size of large walnuts. You should get about 24–28. Place them on a board or plate in a single layer and sift flour on them. Roll them so they are coated in flour all over. Heat the remaining oil in the frying pan and fry the meatballs to brown them all over. Now add the tomatoes and bay leaves and oregano, and season lightly with salt and pepper. Cover the pan and cook for about 15 minutes. Serve garnished with chopped parsley or chives. Good with potatoes, pasta, or rice. Serves 4–6.

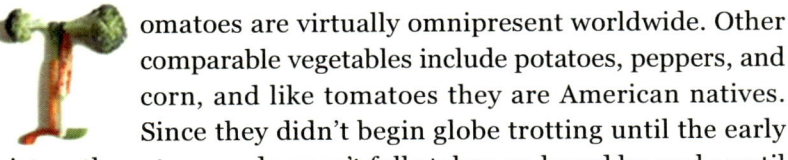

Tomatoes are virtually omnipresent worldwide. Other comparable vegetables include potatoes, peppers, and corn, and like tomatoes they are American natives. Since they didn't begin globe trotting until the early sixteenth century, and weren't fully taken on board by cooks until the eighteenth or even nineteenth century, it's interesting to speculate what pre-Renaissance food must have been like without them. In the case of tomatoes, that would have meant no pizzas and no spaghetti bolognese in Italy, no baked beans in tomato sauce in England, no tomato salads in France and Greece. Though they are classified by the US government as a vegetable, tomatoes are botanically a fruit, and like all fruits they are sweetest and best when just picked. We can buy beautiful tomatoes throughout the year, but for juicy, tomatoey flavor the Valley crop soars way above the supplies we get in winter.

GREEK SALAD

Greek salad is a commonplace on restaurant menus, but it's rarely correctly made. In Greek it's called *horiatiki,* meaning country salad, and so it includes the common vegetables of the

Greek Salad topped with feta for sharing

countryside: tomatoes, onions, peppers, cucumbers – but not lettuce, which does not grow so well in the hot dry climate of Greece. Also Greeks never serve it swamped in an oily dressing. It comes to the table in a bowl, usually glass, topped with a slab of feta, and along with a bottle of oil, which the person charged with the tossing adds immediately before serving.

> *4 ripe tomatoes, sliced or cut in wedges*
> *1–2 green peppers, halved, seeded and sliced*
> *2 unpeeled cucumbers (or 1 if it's a long one), peeled and cut in thick slices*
> *1 small red onion, peeled and sliced*
> *About a dozen black olives*
> *6–8 ounce slice of feta cheese in one piece*
> *1–2 teaspoons dried oregano*
> *Extra-virgin olive oil*

Layer the tomato, green pepper, and cucumber slices in a bowl. Spread the red onion slices into onion circles and put these on top. Scatter on the olives. Place the feta cheese in one or two pieces on top and sprinkle it with oregano. To serve, trickle some extra-virgin olive oil over the feta then toss, breaking the feta into chunks and lightly coating the vegetables with oil. Serves 4.

SPICED TOMATO SALAD

Most of our tomato salads feature herbs such as basil or parsley, and other seasonal vegetables such as cucumber, peppers, and the omnipresent lettuce. This spicy version is a different take on tomato salad – an Indian take featuring favorite Indian spices and flavors. It's perfect with food grilled outdoors, and, of course, Indian foods. Or eat on its own with your favorite bread.

> *1/2 cup balsamic vinegar*
> *1/2 teaspoon black peppercorns*
> *1 teaspoon coriander seeds*
> *1 teaspoon cumin seeds*
> *Seeds from 2 cardamom pods*
> *1 teaspoon powdered allspice*
> *1/4 teaspoon mace*

3 pounds tomatoes of different varieties and colors
1 tablespoon chopped fresh ginger
*1 small chili pepper, seeds discarded and finely
   chopped (optional)*
*6–7 Thai or regular basil leaves, torn plus sprigs
   for garnish*
2 tablespoons coarsely chopped cilantro
2 tablespoons olive oil
Maldon salt or coarse sea salt

Simmer the balsamic vinegar in a small pan until it has reduced to half its volume. Set aside. Spread the peppercorns, coriander seeds, cumin seeds, and cardamom seeds in a small dry frying pan and heat them over gentle heat until they are fragrant – about 1 minute. Grind them by crushing them in a pestle and mortar or whizzing them in a spice grinder. Stir in the allspice powder and mace. Cut large tomatoes in chunks and halve small ones. Put them in a single layer on a large serving platter and scatter the spice mixture on them. Turn them gently. Add the chopped ginger and the chili pepper if you are using it, along with the torn basil leaves and the cilantro. Just before serving drizzle on the vinegar and the olive oil, sprinkle with a little Maldon or sea salt, and scatter on basil sprigs. Serves 6–8 or more.

TOMATO MONKFISH AND POTATO CASSEROLE

This dish comes from Andalucia in southern Spain, where monkfish is a favorite. The fish and vegetables cook together making preparation and clean up easy. You can also make it with other firm-fleshed dish such as chunks of swordfish or halibut.

Large pinch saffron
2 pounds monkfish
salt and white pepper to taste
1–2 tablespoons flour
4 tablespoons olive oil
1 medium onion, chopped
3–4 cups peeled, diced tomatoes
5 medium potatoes, peeled and sliced
1 red or yellow pepper, seeded and cut into thin strips

Put the saffron in a small bowl and cover with half a teacup of warm water. Let it sit for a couple of hours, stirring occasionally to release the color and aroma. When ready to proceed, cut the monkfish into 2-inch chunks, season them with salt and white pepper, and then dust lightly with flour. Heat 3 tablespoons of the olive oil in a sauté pan over medium heat, and cook the monkfish briefly until it is light gold. Remove it from the pan. Cook the onions in the same oil for 3–4 minutes, and then add the tomatoes, potato slices, the saffron and its liquid, and salt and pepper. Pour in enough water to cover the vegetables; bring to a boil, then simmer for 15 minutes or until the potatoes are beginning to soften. Return the monkfish to the pan and cook for another 5–7 minutes. Adjust the seasoning if necessary. Meanwhile gently cook the pepper strips for 5–6 minutes in the remaining oil. Place them on top of the casserole and serve. Serves 4–5.

TOMATO PANCAKES

This recipe comes from an early twentieth-century community cookbook. Tomatoes sound odd in breakfast pancakes, but remember, like the more typical blueberries, tomatoes are a fruit, and bring their own color and flavor to the breakfast table.

1 cup chopped, peeled and seeded tomatoes
2 eggs beaten
1–1 1/2 cups milk
2 teaspoons dried oregano
2 cups all-purpose flour
1 tablespoon sugar
2 teaspoons baking powder
1 teaspoon salt
1–2 tablespoons light flavored oil

Preheat the oven to 250 degrees. Stir together the tomatoes, eggs, 1 cup of milk, and the oregano. In a large bowl, mix the flour, sugar, baking powder, and salt. Make a well in the center and stir in the tomato mixture, stirring to make a thick smooth batter that pours slowly from a pitcher. If necessary add extra milk to achieve this. Grease a griddle with the oil and set over high heat. When it is hot, lower the heat to medium and pour on portions of batter to form pancakes about 4 inches in diameter. Flip the pancakes when the edges are dry and the centers still a little moist – about 3–4 minutes. Cook the second side for 3 minutes. Keep warm in the preheated oven while you continue making pancakes with the rest of the batter. Serves 4.

CHINESE-STYLE STIR-FRIED BEEF AND TOMATOES

When I was a student in Yorkshire Chinese restaurants were still a fairly new phenomenon in the region. Dinner was just within a student budget, and it seemed very adventurous. A stir-fry of beef and tomatoes was a favorite with my friends and me, and we assumed it was a typical Chinese dish. But I have never seen it on the menu of any other Chinese restaurant, so I suspect it was the invention of a cook enthralled with the flavorful supply of tasty tomatoes imported from Holland on the other shore of the North Sea. I still make this when the Valley's tomatoes are in season.

1 tablespoon corn starch
1/2 cup soy sauce
1/2 cup Chinese or Japanese rice wine
1/4 teaspoon allspice
1 pound sandwich steaks cut into 1/4-wide strips
1 tablespoon oil
1 medium onions, finely chopped
1 clove garlic, minced
2-inch pieces fresh ginger cut in thin matchsticks
4–5 firm but ripe small or medium tomatoes, cut into wedge-shaped pieces
8 scallions, white and pale green parts coarsely chopped
1/4 teaspoon white pepper

In a large bowl, mix the cornstarch into a thin paste with 1–2 tablespoons of cold water. Stir in the soy sauce and rice wine. (If rice wine is unobtainable use 1/4 cup sherry plus 1/4 cup water).

Stir in the allspice and then the sandwich steak strips. Let stand for at least 30 minutes and preferably 60 minutes. When you're ready to cook, heat the oil in a wok or deep frying pan until it is slightly shimmery then add the onions and garlic and stir briskly for a minute. Keeping the heat high, stir in the ginger for 30 seconds, then dump in the beef and soy mixture. Let it sizzle, then stir briskly for a minute, before adding the tomatoes and scallions. Let them cook until just heated through – about 2 minutes. Finally stir in the white pepper. Transfer to a heated platter and garnish with the chopped chives. Serves 4.

GREEN ZEBRA SOUP WITH HERBS

Many heirloom tomato varieties now show up in farmers' markets. They come in shades of yellow, orange, and brown, and in shapes that vary from pretty gold tear-drops to lumpy brownish globes. Green Zebra are a medium-sized tomato striped in shades of green. They are often classed as heirlooms, but in fact are a relatively new hybrid that grows easily in local gardens. Since they stay green when ripe they make a tomato soup that looks distinctly different.

> *2 pounds Green Zebra tomatoes*
> *1 tablespoon olive oil*
> *1 medium onion, peeled and chopped*
> *1 medium celery stalk, washed and chopped*
> *5 cups chicken or vegetable stock*
> *1 large sprig of about 6 leaves basil, plus 3–4 extra leaves*
> *1/2 cup finely chopped parsley*
> *Salt, pepper and sugar to taste*
> *2 tablespoons snipped chives*
> *2–3 tablespoons cornstarch*
> *1/2–1 cup milk*
>
> For serving: *about 1/2 cup heavy cream (optional), 6 tiny basil sprigs*

Wash the tomatoes, cut off the blossom ends, and halve. Put a sieve over a bowl and scoop the seeds out of the tomatoes into it. (It doesn't matter if you don't get every last one of them.) Discard the seeds but keep the juice collected in the bowl. Heat the oil in a large pan, and gently cook the onion and celery in it for 3–4 minutes. Stir in the tomatoes, their juice and then the stock. Add the large sprig of basil and about a third of the parsley. Season lightly with salt and pepper, cover the pan and simmer for about 15–20 minutes, or until the tomatoes are tender. Let cool to lukewarm, then process in batches in a food processor or put through a food mill. Pour into a clean pan. Add another third of the parsley and chives, and simmer over medium heat for 3 minutes. Taste and add more salt and pepper and about 1 tablespoon of sugar or less or more to taste. Mix 2 tablespoons of cornstarch with enough cold water to make a smooth thin paste. Add a ladleful of the simmering soup, then pour this mixture into the pan and bring to the boil. If the soup is still thinnish, make up the remaining tablespoon of cornstarch in the same way. Cook until the soup has thickened and then stir in the milk and remaining parsley and chives.

Pour into soup bowls or plates for serving. If you like, pour in a splash of cream holding the container high above the soup so you get a squiggly pattern. Add a tiny sprig of basil to each serving if you have them. Alternately, reserve a little of the chopped parsley and sprinkle it on. Serves 4.

TOMATO AND WINTER SQUASH CHUTNEY

This tawny chutney studded with golden pieces of squash looks intriguing. If you have enough tomatoes and squash make extra to give as holiday gifts.

1 large butternut squash or pumpkin weighing
   about 2 1/2 pounds
1 pound (about 3 large) peeled and seeded tomatoes
1 large onion, peeled and chopped
3 cloves garlic, peeled and minced
3/4 cup golden raisins

1/2 cup crystallized ginger, chopped (optional)
1 1/2 cups white sugar
1 cup dark brown sugar
1/2 teaspoon coarsely ground black pepper
1/2 teaspoon powdered cinnamon
2 teaspoons powdered allspice
1 tablespoon powdered ginger
1 tablespoon salt
3 cups white cider vinegar

Peel the squash and discard the seeds and stringy fibers around them. Cut it into 1-inch cubes. Put the cubes into a large pan such as a pasta pan. Add the other ingredients in the order in which they appear in the recipe. Put the pan on low heat and bring to the boil, stirring occasionally to distribute the ingredients. Raise the heat under the pan and let the mixture boil fairly quickly, stirring from time to time. Do not cover with a lid. After about an hour the liquid will be much diminished and the chutney will be thickening. Watch carefully and stir often to prevent it sticking. You may taste it at this point and add more salt, pepper, sugar, or ginger if you think it needs it. When the mixture reaches a thick jammy consistency it is done.

Pack the chutney in sterilized jars (See page xii). Leave half an inch space at the top of the jar so the chutney doesn't touch the lid. This chutney does not need canning in a water bath because it has a large amount of preservatives in the form of vinegar, sugar and salt. Keep in a cold spot and eat within 2 months.

Other recipes: Cauliflower Gratin with Tomatoes, page 38; Braised Fennel with Mussels, Tomatoes and Rosemary page 59; Ratatouille, page 146; Pisto, page 148; and Minestrone, page 149.

Zucchini was the darling of the seventies and the early eighties, when the enthusiasm for homesteading taught people that one zucchini plant can produce dozens of zucchinis. A part was also played by writers who specialized in vegetarian recipes because they developed scores of ways of using zucchini in soups, vegetable stews, and in baked goods such as breads and muffins. This myriad of uses derives from the zucchini's tenderness, which lets it merge with other ingredients, and its mild – even negligible – taste that lets snazzier ingredients flaunt themselves. On its own, zucchini is best cooked with butter or olive oil – or a fifty-fifty mix of both – and tossed with spritely herbs such as mint, parsley, thyme, or basil. Zucchini grow quickly, but tastes most delicately interesting when they are just 3–4 inches long.

MEXICAN ZUCCHINI WITH CREAM

The French and English call zucchinis *courgettes,* and the Spanish and Mexicans call them *calabacita*. We use the Italian word 'zucchini' so it's no surprise that most of our zucchini recipes follow the Italian practice of flavouring it with herbs. Mexicans often go for spices instead, so their zucchini dishes taste distinctly different from those we know best. The following dish follows suggestions made by Diana Kennedy in her book *The Cuisines of Mexico* (Harper& Row, 1972). In particular, she recommends leaving the pepper whole so that it just flavors the zucchini, "It should not be *picante*," she writes. Of course, if you want a fiery dish you could cut the jalapeño in the following recipe in very thin strips before adding it. Mexicans grow many sorts of zucchini, and often use them in combination. Cream or cheese velvets this dish, and if an extra chili should make its way into the mixture, they also soothe seared tastebuds.

Z

Zucchini, eggplant and more at the market

4–5 zucchini or 2 each zucchini and summer squash, each about 6 inches (total weight about 1 1/2 pounds)
1 large tomato, peeled, seeded and coarsely chopped
8–10 mint leaves, torn in pieces
4 whole cloves
Small cinnamon stick
12 black peppercorns
1 jalapeño
1/2 cup heavy cream
1 cup corn kernels
Salt to taste
Leaves from 1–2 sprigs of cilantro
1/2 cup grated Swiss cheese (optional)

Wash the zucchini (and summer squash if using), trim off the ends and cut into 1-inch pieces. Put these in a saucepan with the tomato, mint, cloves, cinnamon stick, and peppercorns. Add a couple of tablespoons of water and bury the jalapeño in the middle. Season lightly with salt. Cover and cook over low heat for about 10 minutes or until the vegetables have softened. Now add the corn and cream. Continue simmering for another 20 minutes, stirring occasionally and checking to make sure the mixture does not dry out. If it seems to be doing so, add a little more water or cream. When the vegetables are soft and the cream is all absorbed, remove the pepper if you left it whole, tip the contents of the pan into a dish and scatter on the cilantro. Also scatter on the cheese if you like. Serves 6.

ZUCCHINI WITH OLIVE OIL AND LEMON JUICE

As a side dish zucchini can be dispiriting, arriving at the table wet, seedy, and with little to say for itself. This Greek way of cooking them whole preserves their flavor, and the last-minute dressing of olive oil and lemon is just right.

6 zucchini, each about 3–4 inches long
1 teaspoon salt
Extra-virgin olive oil
1 lemon, halved

Put the zucchini in a shallow pan into which they fit in a single layer. Pour on enough boiling water to completely cover them, add the salt, and simmer for about 8 minutes or until they feel tender when probed with a fork. Remove them to a serving dish and line them up in a row. Bring them to the table, and then slice across them at 1-inch intervals so that you cut through all of them in one go. Trickle olive oil generously on top, and squeeze on the lemon juice. Alternately cut the lemon in six wedges, and serve with the zucchini. Serves 4–6.

IRAQI ZUCCHINI CAKE WITH CARDOMOM

This recipe is adapted from one in *The Iraqi Cookbook* written by Lamees Ibrahim and published by Northampton publisher, Interlink Books, which produces many books, cookbooks among them, about the culture of other countries, especially those in the Middle East. This cake is moist and keeps well in an airtight box. Serve it for dessert with a dusting of confectioners' sugar. A scoop of vanilla ice cream makes it extra special,

> *4 eggs*
> *3/4 cup canola or other light-flavored oil*
> *2 cups all-purpose flour*
> *2 teaspoons baking powder*
> *1/2 teaspoon baking soda*
> *1 1/2 cups light brown sugar*
> *1 teaspoon powdered cardamom*
> *3/4 teaspoon cinnamon*
> *1/2 teaspoon nutmeg*
> *2 cups grated zucchini (about 3 zucchini) grated to yield 2 cups, or substitute summer squash*
> *1 cup golden raisins*
> *1 cup walnut pieces*
> *1–2 tablespoons confectioner's sugar*

Preheat the oven to 350 degrees and grease a 9-inch square baking pan or line it with baking parchment. Beat the eggs and oil together until thoroughly blended. In large mixing bowl stir together the flour, baking powder, baking soda, sugar, cardamom, cinnamon, and nutmeg. Make a hollow in the center and stir in the grated zucchini then the egg-and-oil mixture. Mix thoroughly, and finally stir in the golden raisins and walnuts. Pour the mixture into the prepared pan and bake in the center of the preheated oven for 40–50 minutes, or until a toothpick or skewer poked into the center comes out clean. Makes 12 servings.

Other recipes: Zucchini are a basic vegetable in Ratatouille, page 146 and Spanish Pisto, page 148. Use them also in Minestrone, page 149.

Omnium Gatherum

An alphabetically arranged cookbook such as this one creates a problem for itself. Under which letter should dishes that feature two or more vegetables be classified? Rather arbitrarily the problem of the two-vegetable dishes has been to put them under the initial of whichever one seems most important, or where they seem most likely to catch a reader's eye. But some dishes have a multitude of vegetables, none of them pre-eminent. Here we have recipes for six such dishes. They are perfect when we are revelling in late-summer abundance because they don't insist on precise quantities of things, and while each dish has signature ingredients that must be included, other vegetables, if available, can be added too.

MOROCCAN SEVEN-VEGETABLE TAGINE

Couscous aux sept legumes – Couscous with Seven Vegetables – is a classic Moroccan dish. Having seven vegetables is lucky so make sure you have the right number. Onions, tomatoes, and hot peppers don't count – Moroccans consider them as flavoring – so you will end up with ten vegetables in total. The following recipe has 9 (plus the onions, tomatoes, and peppers) so you can pick whichever seven you want – or substitute whatever you like because it doesn't matter which vegetables you use as long as you stick to the magic number. If you have a tagine – the elegant pointy-lidded Moroccan baking dish – use it for this dish. Otherwise a saucepan is fine.

> 2 pounds lamb leg or stew beef cut in chunks
> 2 teaspoons ground ginger
> 2 teaspoons turmeric
> 2 teaspoons black or white pepper
> 1 teaspoon cinnamon
> Salt to taste
> 1 large onion, cut in quarters and thinly sliced.
> 1 small hot pepper, seeded and chopped
> 4 tomatoes, peeled, seeded and chopped

4 carrots, peeled and sliced
4 purple-top turnips, peeled and cut into wedges
1 pound small potatoes, peeled and left whole or halved
6 stalks of celery, cut into 3-inch lengths
1–2 green peppers, seeded and sliced
2 cups cabbage or Swiss Chard chopped into 2-inch strips
1 medium butternut squash, peeled, seeded and cut into 3-inch chunks
2 zucchini, sliced
1 15-ounce can chickpeas, drained
1/2 cup chopped cilantro

Put the lamb or beef in a pot or a tagine. Sprinkle on the spices and season with salt. Add the sliced onion. Cover with water, and simmer for 1 1/2 hours or until the meat is falling-apart tender. Add more water as the original liquid evaporates. Add the hot pepper and tomatoes, and cook for 5 minutes. Now add all the other vegetables you are using except the zucchini, squash, and chickpeas. Cover and simmer for 20 minutes. Now add the zucchini, squash, and chickpeas. Check for seasoning and add salt if necessary. Cover and simmer for another 15 minutes or until everything is tender. During this time prepare couscous according to the package directions. Serve straight from the tagine with couscous on the side, or arrange the couscous in a shallow dish, put the meat on top and the vegetables round the edge. Garnish with cilantro. Serves 6–8.

RATATOUILLE

Ratatouille has become a Valley favorite because our hot summers are like those of Provence, the homeland of ratatouille in southern France. We can grow perfect eggplant, zucchini, tomatoes, and peppers, which are the vital ingredients. Recipes for ratatouille vary tremendously: some have more eggplant, others have more zucchini or tomatoes; potatoes are occasionally added. Exact amounts of each ingredient are never important; ratatouille almost always tastes delicious. Looks and texture are different matters. Despite vivid tomatoes and peppers, lengthy cooking with eggplant can produce a brown mush. It's not surprising that the authoritative *Larousse Gastronomique* says that the word '*ratatouille*' first meant an "unappetizing stew." Worsening the brown-mush problem, the Valley's summer rains make our vegetables juicier than those of the Mediterranean, and all that juice can require evaporation by bubbling it away – a process that increases mushifcation. The following recipe offers several stratagems to deal with these problems. To keep the colors as bright as possible, red peppers bump out green and yellow summer squash substitutes for some of the zucchini because it hold its shape and color better. The zucchini, summer squash, and eggplant are salted to get rid of some of their natural liquid before it has a chance to swill around your pan and demand evaporation. Plum tomatoes are used because they are fleshier. Starting things off in separate pans also helps because they can cook at their own speed. This ratatouille delights with both the sumptuous softness that is the hallmark of this dish, and entices also with splashes of summer-vegetable color. (Illustrated on back cover.)

> *1 pound (1 large) eggplant, washed and cut in cubes*
> *3/4 pound (about 2–3) summer squash, washed and thickly sliced*
> *1/2 pound (about 2–3) zucchini, washed and thickly sliced*
> About 2 tablespoons salt
> *6–8 tablespoons olive oil or more as needed*

2 large onions, peeled and chopped
3–4 large garlic cloves peeled and minced
1 pound (about 5–6) large plum tomatoes, peeled and seeded
2 red peppers, washed and cut in strips
2 teaspoons whole coriander seeds
1 teaspoon dried oregano or thyme
8 large basil leaves plus 2–3 nice sprigs for garnish

Put the unpeeled and cubed eggplant and zucchini slices into a large colander. Add the summer squash slices, keeping them to one side of the colander so you can get them out later. Sprinkle the salt on them. Place a plate directly on top and weight it down with cans of food. Leave standing in the sink for 45 minutes. Rinse off the salt with cold water, then dry the vegetables with a kitchen towel. Separate the summer squash and reserve.

In a large wide pan heat 3 tablespoons of the olive oil, put in the eggplant and zucchini and cook over low heat, stirring to distribute the oil. Add another tablespoonful if you don't have enough to moisten everything. Cover the pan and let cook gently, stirring occasionally for about 20 minutes. Add the summer squash and continue cooking for another 15–20 minutes or until the pieces are tender but not collapsing.

Meanwhile in a frying pan heat another 2 tablespoons of olive oil over moderate heat. Add the chopped onions and garlic, and cook for 5–6 minutes until they have softened slightly. Now chop the tomatoes and stir them into the onions. Cook for 2–3 minutes, then add the red pepper strips. Season lightly with salt. Crush the coriander seeds with a pestle or a rolling pin, add half of them, the oregano or thyme, and 4 torn basil leaves. Cover the pan and cook for 15 minutes, or until the pepper strips are tender.

When both mixtures are tender, add the tomato-pepper mixture to the eggplant mixture. Stir in the remaining coriander and torn basil leaves. Cover and cook for 5–10 minutes or until the flavors are blended. Serve with the basil sprigs as garnish. Ratatouille is excellent hot or warm with roast chicken or lamb or grilled meats, and good also cold with bread or cheeses. Serves 8.

SPANISH PISTO

Pisto is a Spanish cousin of ratatouille, and it comes in many forms. Sometimes the vegetables are cut in chunks as for ratatouille; but often they are chopped into tiny confetti-size dice. They are cooked until tender but not mushy, and eggs are often added, either stirred in as in this recipe, or fried and served on top. Pisto sometimes appears at room temperature in tapas bars. It can also be served warm as a side dish. Quantities of each vegetable vary depending on what's available.

> 4 tablespoons olive oil
> 1 large onion, diced small
> 1 clove garlic, finely minced
> 2 green or red peppers, diced small
> 1 medium eggplant, peeled and diced small
> Salt and pepper to taste
> 6 medium ripe but not over-ripe tomatoes, peeled,
>   seeded and diced small
> 1 zucchini or summer squash, diced small
> 1 egg beaten with a tablespoon of milk
> 1/3 cup chopped parsley eggs beaten with 1
>   tablespoon milk

Heat the oil in a shallow pan. Soften the onion, garlic and peppers in it, then add the eggplant and cook until the oil has been absorbed and the eggplant has softened. Season, then add the tomatoes and zucchini or summer squash. Cover the pan and cook for about 5 minutes over a low heat. Remove the lid and increase the heat to evaporate all but 3–4 tablespoons of the juices. Taste and season again if necessary. Off the heat rapidly stir in the egg mixture until it sets into small fragments. (For an eggier dish, make 4 hollows in the mixture, drop an egg into each one, cover and cook until the yolk has set.) Sprinkle on the parsley and serve. Serves 4–6.

MINESTRONE

Minestrone requires tomatoes and some other basic vegetables plus anything else that's available. Thus a minestrone made in August may have green beans, summer squash, and broccoli, but one made in late-September or October may have winter squash, leeks, and cabbage. This recipe lists the basic ingredients first, followed by a list of options – and feel free to add to these. Minestrone freezes well and it's a delight to eat in the middle of winter when each vegetable will recall the garden where you grew it or the farmstand where you bought it. However, if you plan to freeze it, don't add the pasta before it goes into the freezer because freezing messes it up. Include it when you reheat the soup for serving.

Basic Ingredients:

2 tablespoons olive oil
1 large onion, chopped
2–3 cloves garlic, minced
1–2 stems celery, chopped
1–2 carrots, peeled and chopped
4 large ripe tomatoes (about 1 1/2 pounds), peeled, seeded, and chopped
Salt and pepper to taste
1 bay leaf
6 torn basil leaves
1 tablespoon chopped fresh oregano or 1 teaspoon dried
4–6 cups vegetable or chicken stock
1/2 cup small pasta shape such as orzo or tiny shells
Grated Parmesan for serving

Other possible ingredients:

Piece of parmesan rind
Purple-top turnips, peeled and diced
Potatoes, peeled and diced
Green or red peppers, seeded and diced

Green beans, trimmed and cut in 1-inch pieces
Green peas
Swiss chard, stems and leaves separated, chopped
Spinach leaves, chopped if large
Summer squash or zucchini, or both
White or Savoy cabbage, chopped
Leeks, washed and cut in circles
*Cooked or canned chickpeas, cannellini or pinto
   beans*
Broccoli, broken into florets

Heat the oil in a large pan and gently cook the onions, garlic, celery, and carrot in it for 4–5 minutes, stirring occasionally. Stir in the tomaotes, bay leaf, basil, oregano, and a light seasoning of salt and pepper. Cover the pan and cook gently until the tomatoes have softened. Now add 2 cups of stock and other vegetables. Begin by adding hard vegetables that take longer to cook such as potatoes and purple-top turnips along with Parmesan rind if you have it. When these begin to soften add any peppers, green beans or peas, Swiss chard stems, hard white cabbage, leeks and cooked or canned beans. After a few minutes add softer vegetables such as zucchini, broccoli, spinach, and torn Swiss chard leaves. Add more stock (or water) if you think it necessary. About 10 minutes before you plan to serve the soup add the pasta shapes. Serves 6–10.

PICALLILI

Picallili is an end-of-season mustard pickle from England. Cucumber and cauliflower should predominate, but other vegetables are always included depending on what's available. People who have tomato plants commonly include the last green tomatoes. Red pepper is popular for the specks of scarlet it adds to the yellow mixture. Peas, green beans, carrots, purple-top turnips, and even Swiss chard stems all may appear. Everything must be chopped into tiny dice.

Vegetables:

1 1/2–2 pounds vegetables including:
about 10 ounces peeled cucumber (about 2–3 cups diced)
about 6 ounces small cauliflower florets (about 1 cup)
6 ounces diced green tomato (about 3/4 cup)
1 carrot, peeled
1 red bell pepper, diced
few peas or green beans (optional)
4–5 chard stalks, washed and diced (optional)
1 medium purple-top turnip, peeled and diced (optional)
1/3 cup salt

Pickle mixture:

2 tablespoons cornstarch
1 tablespoon English or Chinese mustard powder
2 teaspoons powdered ginger
1 teaspoon powdered turmeric
1/2 teaspoon allspice
2 cups white cider vinegar
1/2 cup sugar

Dice the vegetables small. The carrot should be peeled, cut longways into quarters, which should be thinly sliced. Peas need no cutting but green beans should be cut into pea-sized bits. Put the cut vegetables into a shallow nonreactive dish such as a glass Pyrex lasagne pan and sprinkle with the salt. Cover with plastic wrap and leave for 12–18 hours, by which time the salt will have dissolved and the vegetables will be sitting in brine. Rinse them, then dump them into a large bowl of cold water and swish them vigorously around. Drain thoroughly, then repeat this process two more times.

In a large saucepan stir together the cornstarch, mustard powder, ginger, turmeric, and allspice. Add about a quarter cup of the vinegar and stir into a smooth paste. Stir in the rest of the vinegar, and put the pan over a moderate heat. Stir until the mixture thickens, then stir in the sugar and finally the drained vegetables. Simmer, stirring often, for 10–15 minutes, or until the vegetables are tender. Pour into sterilized jars (see page xii) and seal. You do not need to can picallili that you plan to eat within 4–6 weeks because it has a lot of preservatives in the form of vinegar, salt, and sugar. Makes about 1 quart.

INDEX

Acorn Squash 1-4
    Acorn Squash with Cumin-Perfumed Lamb and Lentils, 1
    Acorn Squash with Sage and Apple Stuffing and Pecans, 3
Acton, Eliza, *Modern Cookery,* 67
Adam's Luxury and Eve's Cookery, (Anon), 75
Afghanistan, 30
America, American, 52, 62, 66, 86, 92, 99, 125, 132
Amherst, 84
Anglesey, 71
    Anglesey Eggs, 71
Apple
    Acorn Squash with Sage and Apple Stuffing and Pecans, 3
    Butternut Sautéed with Apples and Onion, 23
Apricot
    Pumpkin Caramel Custard with Spiced Apricots, 107
Arab, Arabian, 49, 52-53,
Arugula, 4-5
    Arugula and Pears with Blue Cheese, 5
    Greek Arugula and Carrot Salad with Capers and Olives, 4
Asparagus, 6-10, asparagus ice cream, 6
    Asparagus in Jackets, 6
    Asparagus with Chiveblossom Vinaigrette, 7
    Asparagus and Ham Gratin, 10
    Salmon and Asparagus Bisque, 8
Australia, 129

Bacon, 29, 62, 114
    Maltese Cabbage with Bacon, 29
    Rutabaga and Potato Cake with Bacon, 114
Balsamic Vinegar
    Broccoli Rabe with Balsamic Vinegar and Cranberries, 17
Barley, 102
    Beet and Barley Risotto, 13
Barron, Rosemary, *Flavors of Greece,* 56
Bay leaves
    Eggplants with Feta and Bay Leaves, 56
Beef
    Chinese-Style Stir-Fried Beef and Tomatoes, 136
    Keema Curry with Peas, 87
    Sirloin Tips Braised with Peas and Mushrooms, 88
Beets, 11-14, horseradish with beets, 11
    Baby Beet Salad, 12
    Beet and Barley Risotto, 13
    Roasted Beets with Lemon and Dill, 11
Blue cheese, x
    Arugula and Pears with Blue Cheese, 5

Bread,
    Pumpkin Bread with Cranberries, 105
Britain, 18, 29, 32
Broccoli, 14-18
    Broccoli and Cheddar Soup, 14
    Broccoli Cream, 15
    Broccoli, Red Pepper and Rosemary Quiche, 16
    Stir-Fried Chicken with Snowpeas and Broccoli, 89
Broccoli Rabe, 17-18
    Broccoli Rabe with Balsamic Vinegar and Cranberries, 17
Bruschetta
    Slit Leeks Bruschetta, 73
Brussels Sprouts, 18-20
    Brussels Sprouts with Chestnuts and Nutmeg, 18
    Soup of Brussels Sprouts with Golden Sippets, 19
Butternut Squash, 21- 25, butternut coconut soup, 22
    Butternut Caribé, 21
    Butternut Fries, 24
    Butternut and Peanut Soup, 22
    Butternut Sautéed with Apples and Onions, 23

Cabbage, 26-29
    Colcannon, 26
    Far I Kal, 27
    Maltese Cabbage with Bacon, 29
    Rabbit Braised with Cabbage and Carrots, 28
Capers
    Greek Arugula and Carrot Salad with Capers and Olives, 4
Cape Cod, 66, 97
Caponata, 53
Caraway,
    Onion and Caraway Cobbler, 82
Cardamom
    Iraqi Zucchini Cake with Cardomom, 143
Caribbean, 21, 92
    Butternut Caribé, 21
Carrot, 30-36
    Braised Carrots and Leeks, 31
    Carrot and Pineapple Cake, 34
    Carrot and Mint Pilaf, 33,
    Chopped Carrots and Swede, 32
    Greek Arugula and Carrot Salad with Capers and Olives, 4
    Mexican Carrot and Cucumber Sticks, 30
    Mustard-Mint Carrots, 31
    Rabbit Braised with Cabbage and Carrots, 28
Casserole
    Eggplant and Lamb Casserole, 55
    Mushroom and Chicken Casserole, 78
    Rabbit Braised with Cabbage and Carrots, 28

Index

Tomato, Monkfish and Potato Casserole, 134
Cauliflower, 36-40, 151
    Cauliflower Gratin with Tomatoes, 38
    Classic Cauliflower Cheese, 36
Indian-Style Cauliflower with Potatoes, 39
Celeriac, 40-42
    Celeriac Soup with Scallops, 41
Champlain, Samuel, 66
Cheddar, x-xi
    Broccoli and Cheddar Soup, 14
Cheese, x-xi
    Arugula and Pears with Blue Cheese, 5
    Broccoli and Cheddar Soup, 14
    Cheese Sauce, xi
    Cheese-Stuffed Squash Blossoms, 122
Chestnuts
    Brussels Sprouts with Chestnuts and Nutmeg, 18
Chicken
    Chicken with Corn and Cider, 44
    Moroccan-Style Chicken with Jerusalem Artichokes, 68
    Mushroom and Chicken Casserole, 78
    Stir-Fried Chicken with Snowpeas and Broccoli, 89
Chili
    Chili with Multicolored Peppers, 96
China, Chinese, 78, 89, 92, 133
    Chinese-Style Stir-Fried Beef and Tomatoes, 136
    Stir-Fried Chicken with Snowpeas and Broccoli, 89
Chiveblossom
    Asparagus with Chiveblossom Vinaigrette, 7
Chowder
    Corn, Leek and Salmon Chowder, 44
Christmas, 18
Chutney
    Green Bean Chutney, 65
    Tomato and Winter Squash Chutney, 138
Cider
    Chicken with Corn and Cider, 44
Cieslik, Nikki, 43
Citrus fruit, x, *(See also specific fruit such as lemon, orange)*
Cobbler
    Onion and Caraway Cobbler, 82
Colcannon, 26
Coconut, 22
Cook, Beth, 6
Coriander
    Delicata Boats Laden with Orange-Coriander Orzo, 50
Corn, 42-45
    Chicken with Corn and Cider, 44
    Corn, Leek and Salmon Chowder, 44

Grilled Corn, 42
Margarita Corn Salsa, 43
Twice-Baked Potatoes with Tuna and Corn, 103
Coriander
    Delicata Boats Laden with Orange-Coriander Orzo, 51
Cracow, 101
Cranberry, 17, 97, 105
    Broccoli Rabe with Balsamic Vinegar and Cranberries, 17
    Pumpkin Bread with Cranberries, 105
Croatia, 129
Croquette
    Potato Croquettes with Rosemary, 100
Cucumber, 45-49, 151
    Cucumber Sandwiches, 47
    Dr. Johnson's Cucumber Pickle, 48
    Flower by the Wayside Curry of Cucumber and Shrimp, 46
    Mexican Carrot and Cucumber Sticks, 30
    Tzatziki, 49
Culinary Jottings for Madras (Colonel A. Kenney-Herbert), 46
Curd
    Pumpkin Curd, 106
Curry
    Curried Parsnip Soup, 85
    Flower by the Wayside Curry of Cucumber and Shrimp, 46
    Keema Curry with Peas, 87

Deerfield, 31, 43, 53
Delicata Squash, 50-51
    Delicata Boats Laden with Orange-Coriander Orzo, 51
Diat, Louis, 74
Dill, 11, 79
    Roasted Beets with Lemon and Dill, 11
    Russian-Style Mushrooms with Sour Cream and Dill, 79

Egg, xi-xii, 71
    Anglesey Eggs, 71
    Mushroom Frittata with Ham and Peas, 80
Eggplant, 52-56
    Caponata, 53
    Eggplant with Feta and Bay Leaves, 56
    Eggplant and Lamb Casserole, 55
    Stockbridge Farm No-Fry Eggplant, 52
England, English, 4-5, 18, 32, 46, 47, 48, 52, 84, 132, 140, 151
    Chopped Carrot and Swede, 32
    Cucumber Sandwiches, 47
    Dr. Johnson's Cucumber Pickle, 48
    Piccalilli, 151
    Roast Parsnips, 84

Index

Far I Kal, 27
Fennel, 57-60
    Braised Fennel with Mussels, Tomatoes and Rosemary, 59
    Fennel with Pasta, Seafood and Saffron Cream, 58
Potato, Fennel and Leek Gratin, 102
Feta, x
    Eggplant with Feta and bay Leaves, 56
Fiddleheads, 60-61, 90
Fiddler's Pantry, (South Congregational Church, Amherst), 84
Flavors of Greece (Rosemary Barron), 56
Flayvors of Cook's Farm, 6
Flowers
    Asparagus with Chiveblossom Vinaigrette, 7
    Cheese-Stuffed Squash Blossoms, 122
    Flowery Salad with Lavender-Lime Dressing, 76
Food Combining for Health: A New Look at the Hay System (Doris Grant and Jean Joice), 38
Forme of Cury, (Anon), 73
France, French, 52, 66, 74, 78, 86, 109, 111, 121, 129, 132, 140, 146
    Ratatouille, 146
Frittata,
    Mushroom Frittata with Ham and Peas, 80

Gerard, John, *Great Herball, or General Historie of Plantes,* 52
Grange, Cyril *The Right Way to Make Jams,* 106
Grant, Doris and Joice, Jean, *Food Combining for Health: A New Look at the Hay System,* 38
Gratin
    Asparagus and Ham Gratin, 10
    Cauliflower Gratin with Tomatoes, 38
    Potato, Fennel and Leek Gratin, 102
Greece, Greek, 4, 12, 49, 63, 132, 142
    Baby Beet Salad, 12
    Greek Arugula and Carrot Salad with Capers and Olives, 4
    Greek Salad, 132
    Green Beans with Olive Oil and Tomatoes, 63
    Tzatziki, 49
    Zucchini with Olive Oil and Lemon Juice, 142
Green Beans, 62-65
    Green Beans with Olive Oil and Tomatoes, 63
    Italian Green Bean Salad, 64
    Green Bean Chutney, 65
Green Zebra Soup with Herbs, 137

Hadley, 6, 9, 45
Ham
    Asparagus and Ham Gratin, 10
    Mushroom Frittata with Ham and Peas, 80
Halloween, 96

Hanukkah, 101
Herbs, (*See also specific herbs such as such as dill, mint, etc.*)
    Risotto with Sugar-Snap Peas and Spring Herbs, 90
    Green Zebra Soup with Herbs, 137
Horseradish, 11
Hungary, 91

Ibrahim, Lamees, *The Iraqi Cookbook*, 143
India, Indian, v, 5, 30, 33, 39, 49, 65, 92, 133
    Indian-Style Cauliflower with Potatoes, 39
    Keema Curry with Peas, 87
    Spiced Tomato Salad, 133
Indonesia, v
Iraq
    Iraqi Zucchini Cake with Cardomom, 143
Ireland, Irish, 26, 32
    Colcannon, 26
Italy, Italian, iv, 4, 17,29, 52, 53, 57, 64 , 77, 80, 86, 93, 105, 129,
    Caponata, 53
    Italian Bean Salad, 64
    Marinated Pumpkin Slices with Mint, 105
    Mushroom Frittata with Ham and Peas, 80
    Sweet Potatoes and Italian Sausage Sautéed with Summer Vegetables, 128
    Pepperonata, 93

Japan, Japanese, 78, 88, 100, 111-112
    Japanese Pickled Radishes, 112
Jars (sterilizing), xii
Jefferson, Thomas, 52, 57, 86
Jelly
    Hot Red Pepper Jelly, 97
Jerusalem Artichokes, 66-68
    Moroccan-Style Chicken with Jerusalem Artichokes, 68
    Palestine Soup, 67
Johnson, Dr. Samuel, 48
    Dr. Johnson's Cucumber Pickle, 48
Joice, Jean and Doris Grant, *Food Combining for Health: A New Look at the Hay System*, 38

Kale, 26, 69-70
    Portuguese Kale Soup, 69
Keema Curry with Peas, 87
Kennedy, Diana, *The Cuisines of Mexico*, 140
Kenney-Herbert, Colonel A., *Culinary Jottings for Madras*, 46
King Cadwallader (of Wales), 71
King Louis XIV (of France), 86
King Richard II (of England), 73

Index

Lamb
  Acorn Squash with Cumin-Perfumed Lamb and Lentils, 1
  Far I Kal, 27
  Eggplant and Lamb Casserole, 55
Larousse Gastronomique, 146
Latkes, 101
Lavender, 31
  Flowery Salad with Lavender-Lime Dressing, 86
Leeks, 71-75
  Anglesey Eggs, 71
  Braised Carrots and Leeks, 31
  Corn, Leek and Salmon Chowder, 44
  Leek-Filled Yorkshire Pudding, 72
  Potato, Fennel and Leek Gratin, 102
  Slit Leeks Bruschetta, 73
  Vichysoisse, 74
Lemon, x
  Lemon Potatoes, 99
  Roasted Beets with Lemon and Dill, 11
  Greek Zucchini with Olive Oil and Lemon Juice, 142
Lentils
  Acorn Squash with Cumin-Perfumed Lamb and Lentils, 1
  Swiss Chard and Lentil Soup, 129
Lettuce, 75
  Flowery Salad with Lavender-Lime Dressing, 75
Lime, x
Liverpool, 19

Mackerel
  Spaghetti Squash and Smoked Mackerel Salad, 116
Maintenon, Mme. de, 86
Malta, Maltese, 29
  Maltese Cabbage with Bacon, 29
Maple
  Maple-Glazed Turnips, 110
  Radish and Spinach Salad with Maple-Mustard Dressing, 112
Massachusetts, 4, 17, 66, 104
May, Robert, *The Accomplish't Cook,* 23
Meatballs
  Swiss Chard and Pork Meatballs, 130
Mediterranean, 42, 49, 52,122, 126, 146
Mexico, 30, 92, 122, 140-141
  Mexican Carrot and Cucumber Sticks, 30
  Mexican Zucchini with Cream, 140
Middle East, 33, 94, 143
Minestrone, 149
Mint
  Carrot and Mint Pilaf, 33
  Marinated Pumpkin Slices with Mint, 105

Mustard-Mint Carrots, 31
    Pea and Mint Salad, 86
Monkfish
    Tomato, Monkfish and Potato Casserole, 134
Morocco, Moroccan, 68, 144
    Moroccan-Style Chicken with Jerusalem Artichokes, 68
    Moroccan Seven-Vegetable Tagine, 144
Muffins
    Morning Glory Muffins, 125
Mushrooms, 77-81
    Mushroom and Chicken Casserole, 78
    Mushroom Frittata with Ham and Peas, 80
    Russian-Style Mushrooms with Sour Cream and Dill, 79
    Sirloin Tips Braised with Peas and Mushrooms, 88
Mussels
    Braised Fennel with Mussels, Tomatoes and Rosemary, 59
Mustard
    Mustard-Mint Carrots, 31
    Radish and Spinach Salad with Maple-Mustard Dressing, 112

Nabokov, Vladimir 79
Nelson, Irene, 38
North Adams, 88
Norway, 27, 112
    Far I Kal, 27
Nuts ix-ix, *(See also specific nuts such as pecans, etc.)*
Nutmeg, 18, 21
    Brussels Sprouts with Chestnuts and Nutmeg, 18-19

Olives, Olive Oil
    Greek Arugula and Carrot Salad with Capers and Olives, 4
    Green Beans with Olive Oil and Tomatoes, 63
    Greek Zucchini with Olive Oil and Lemon Juice, 142
 Judith Olney *Judith Olney on Bread,* 82
Onion, 81-83
    Butternut Sautéed with Apples and Onions, 23
    Onion and Caraway Cobbler, 82
    Spanish Onion Soup, 83
Orange, vi
    Delicata Boats Laden with Orange-Coriander Orzo, 51
Orzo
    Delicata Boats Laden with Orange-Coriander Orzo, 51

Palestine, 67
    Palestine Soup, 67
Pancake
    Tomato Pancakes, 135
    Latkes, 101

Index

Panko, 100
Parsnip, 84-85
    Curried Parsnip Soup, 85
    Roast Parsnips, 84
Pasta
    Delicata Boats Laden with Orange-Coriander Orzo, 51
    Fennel with Pasta, Seafood and Saffron Cream, 58
Peanut
    Butternut and Peanut Soup, 22
Pea, 86-91
    Keema Curry with Peas, 87
    Mushroom Frittata with Ham and Peas, 80
    Pea and Mint Salad, 86
    Risotto with Sugar-Snap Peas and Spring Herbs, 90
    Sirloin Tips Braised with Peas and Mushrooms, 88
    Stir-Fried Chicken with Snow-peas and Broccoli, 89
Pear
    Arugula and Pears with Blue Cheese, 5
Pecan, ix
    Acorn Squash with Sage and Apple Stuffing and Pecans, 3
Pepper, 92-99
    Broccoli, Red Pepper and Rosemary Quiche, 16
    Chili with Multicolored Peppers, 96
    Hot Red Pepper Jelly, 97
    Pepperonata, 93
    Peppers Stuffed with Raisin and Walnut Pilaf, 94
Peppercorns, viii-x
Pepperonata, 93
Peru, 62
Picallili, 151
Pickle
    Dr. Johnson's Cucumber Pickle, 48
    Japanese Pickled Radishes, 112
    Picallili, 151
Pie
    Sweet Potato Meringue Pie, 127
Pilaf
    Carrot and Mint Pilaf, 33
    Peppers Stuffed with Raisin and Walnut Pilaf, 94
Pineapple
    Carrot and Pineapple Cake, 34
Pine-nuts, ix
Pisto, Spanish, 148
Pittsfield, 124
Poland, Polish, 11, 26, 77, 101
Pork
    Swiss Chard and Pork Meatballs, 130

Portugal, Portuguese
    Portuguese Kale Soup, 69
Potato, 99-104
    Indian-Style Cauliflower with Potatoes, 39-40
    Latkes, 101
    Lemon Potatoes, 99
    Potato Croquettes with Rosemary, 100
    Potato, Fennel and Leek Gratin, 102
    Rutabaga and Potato Cake with Bacon, 114
    Tomato, Monkfish and Potato Casserole, 134
    Twice-Baked Potatoes with Tuna and Corn, 103
Pumpkin, 104-109, 122
    Marinated Pumpkin Slices with Mint, 105
    Pumpkin Bread with Cranberries, 105
    Pumpkin Caramel Custard with Spiced Apricots, 107
    Pumpkin Curd, 106
Purple-Top Turnips, 109-110
    Crumbed Purple Tops, 109
    Maple-Glazed Turnips, 110

Quiche
    Broccoli, Red Pepper and Rosemary Quiche, 16

Rabbit
    Rabbit Braised with Cabbage and Carrots, 28
Radish, 111-113
    Radish and Spinach Salad with Maple-Mustard Dressing, 112
    Japanese Pickled Radishes, 112
Raisin
    Peppers Stuffed with Raisin and Walnut Pilaf, 94
Ratatouille, 146
Risotto, 13, 90
    Beet and Barley Risotto, 13
    Risotto with Sugar-Snap Peas and Spring Herbs, 90
Rogers, James Silas, 113
    Rutabagas: A Love Poem, 113
Rosemary
    Broccoli, Red Pepper and Rosemary Quiche, 16
    Braised Fennel with Mussels, Tomatoes and Rosemary, 59
    Potato Croquettes with Rosemary, 100
Russia, Russian, 77, 79
    Russian-Style Mushrooms with Sour Cream and Dill, 79
Rutabaga, 113-115
    Chopped Carrots and Swede, 32
    Rutabaga and Potato Cake with Bacon, 114
    Vanilla-Scented Rutabaga, 114
Rutabagas: A Love Poem (James Silas Rogers), 113

Index

Saffron
    Fennel with Pasta, Seafood and Saffron Cream, 57, 58
Sage
    Acorn Squash with Sage and Apple Stuffing, 3
Salad
    Baby Beet Salad, 12
    Flowery Salad with Lavender-Lime Dressing, 76
    Greek Arugula and Carrot Salad with Capers and Olives, 4
    Greek Salad, 132
    Italian Green Bean Salad, 64
    Pea and Mint Salad, 86
    Radish and Spinach Salad with Maple-Mustard Dressing, 112
    Spaghetti Squash and Smoked Mackerel Salad, 116
    Spiced Tomato Salad, 133
Salmon
    Salmon and Asparagus Bisque, 8
    Spinach and Salmon Roulade, 118
    Corn, Leek and Salmon Chowder, 44
Salsa
    Margarita Corn Salsa, 43
Sandwich
    Cucumber Sandwiches, 47
Sausage
    Sweet Potatoes and Italian Sausage Sautéed with Summer Vegetables, 128
Scallops
    Celeriac Soup with Scallops, 41-42
Seafood
    Fennel with Pasta, Seafood and Saffron Cream, 57, 58
Shakers, 124
    The Shakers' Heavenly Squash, 124
Shakespeare, William, 75, 125
Shiitake, 78-79
Shrimp
    Flower by the Wayside Curry of Cucumber and Shrimp, 46
Sippets, 19, 73
    Soup of Brussels Sprouts with Golden Sippets, 19
Sirloin Tips
    Sirloin Tips Braised with Peas and Mushrooms, 88
Snowpeas, 86, 90
    Stir-Fried Chicken with Snowpeas and Broccoli, 89
Soup
    Broccoli and Cheddar Soup, 14
    Butternut and Peanut Soup, 22
    Celeriac Soup with Scallops, 40
    Corn, Leek and Salmon Chowder, 44
    Curried Parsnip Soup, 85
    Green Zebra Soup with Herbs, 137
    Minestrone, 149

Palestine Soup, 67
Portuguese Kale Soup, 69
Salmon and Asparagus Bisque, 7
Spanish Onion Soup, 83
Soup of Brussels Sprouts with Golden Sippets, 19
Swiss Chard and Lentil Soup, 129
Vichysoisse, 74
Spaghetti Squash, 116-117
   Spaghetti Squash and Smoked Mackerel Salad, 116
Spain, Spanish, 52, 92, 120, 125, 134, 140, 148
   Spanish Onion Soup, 83
   Spanish Spinach, 120
   Spanish Pisto, 148
   Tomato, Monkfish and Potato Casserole, 134
Spinach, 117-121
   Fish Florentine, 121
   Radish and Spinach Salad with Maple-Mustard Dressing, 112
   Spanish Spinach, 120
   Spinach and Salmon Roulade, 118
Squash blossoms. 122-123
   Cheese-Stuffed Squash Blossoms, 122
   Risotto of Sugar Snap Peas and Spring Herbs, 90
Sri Lanka, 46
   Flower by the Wayside Curry of Cucumber and Shrimp, 46
Sterilizing jars, xii
Sugar-Snap Peas, 86, 90
   Risotto with Sugar-Snap Peas and Spring Herbs, 90
Summer Squash, 123-124
   The Shakers' Heavenly Squash, 124
Sunchoke (Jerusalem artichoke), 67
Sweet Potatoes, 125-129
   Morning Glory Muffins, 125
   Sweet Potatoes and Italian Sausage Sautéed with Summer Vegetables, 128
   Sweet Potato Meringue Pie, 127
Sweden, Swede 32
   Chopped Carrots and Swede, 32
Swiss Chard, 129-131
   Swiss Chard and Lentil Soup, 129
   Swiss Chard and Pork Meatballs, 130
Swift, Jonathan, 6

Tagine
   Moroccan Seven-Vegetable Tagine, 144
Thanksgiving, 104, 127
The Accomplish't Cook (Robert May), 23
The Cuisines of Mexico (Diana Kennedy), 140
The Iraqi Cookbook (Lamees Ibrahim), 143
The Right Way to Make Jams (Cyril Grange) 106

Index

Tomato, 132-139
    Braised Fennel with Mussels, Tomatoes and Rosemary, 59
    Cauliflower Gratin with Tomatoes, 38
    Chinese-Style Stir-Fried Beef and Tomatoes, 136
    Greek Salad, 132
    Green Beans with Olive Oil and Tomatoes, 63
    Green Zebra Soup with Herbs, 137
    Spiced Tomato Salad, 133
    Tomato, Monkfish and Potato Casserole, 134
    Tomato Pancakes, 135
    Tomato and Winter Squash Chutney, 138
Tuna
    Twice-Baked Potatoes with Tuna and Corn, 103
Turkey, Turkish, 49, 129
Turnip, Purple-top, 109-110
    Crumbed Purple-Tops, 109
    Maple-Glazed Turnips, 110
Twain, Mark 36
Tzatziki, 49

Vanilla, 92, 114
    Vanilla-Scented Rutabaga, 114
Vichysoisse, 74

Wales, 70-71
    Anglesey Eggs, 71
Walnut, ix
    Peppers Stuffed with Raisin and Walnut Pilaf, 94
Warchol, Mary Ellen, 31, 52
Warner, Dick, 84
Whately, 43
Winter squash, 122 (*See also specific squashes such as acorn, pumpkin, etc*)
    Tomato and Winter Squash Chutney, 138

Yorkshire, 136
    Leek-Filled Yorkshire Pudding, 72

Zucchini, 122, 140-143
    Iraqi Zucchini Cake with Cardomom, 143
    Mexican Zucchini with Cream, 140
    Zucchini with Olive Oil and Lemon Juice, 142